LIGHT IN THE DARKNESS

LIGHT IN THE DARKNESS

UNCOVERING GRIEF AND TRAUMA

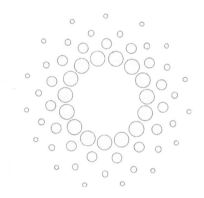

Kimberly Resch and Brian Ross

with CORRINE CASANOVA

Foreword by THOR EELLS

softcover 978-1-7356959-3-8
ebook 978-1-7356959-9-0
hardcover 978-1-7356959-8-3

Cover design by Jody Henning
Illustrations by Kimberly Resch
Interior design by Andrea Reider

Disclaimer: This book discusses real-life trauma and traumatic
events. Reader discretion is advised. This publication is not
intended as a substitute for professional medical or mental health
advice, diagnosis, or treatment. The stories and case studies
shared within this book are from real people. No names or
circumstances have been changed.

CONTENTS

FOREWORD

I had the opportunity to meet Kimberly Resch and Brian Ross several years ago when our paths crossed by chance. A mutual friend introduced us as they knew we both had a shared interest in mental health and its challenges. Within minutes of meeting them, it became apparent that they were passionate and personally invested in solving the mental health epidemic problem. Our business relationship quickly developed into a personal one as well. Over time, I have been amazed at their dedication to making a lasting impact on lifting the stigma of mental illness and how they have unwittingly become a "light in the darkness" for those seeking hope.

Before the COVID-19 pandemic, arguably, the most serious crisis facing this country was the mental illness epidemic. Most of us know someone close to us who is affected by mental illness, and yet it is exceedingly difficult to get mental health care. Sadly, to make matters worse, the topic is often taboo and can be difficult to face because of its stigma. Fortunately, the terms PTS (post-traumatic stress) and PTSD (post-traumatic stress disorder) have helped create more awareness and opportunity to destigmatize mental illness. While our highly regarded veterans and first responders are often associated with these terms, we realize they are not the only ones struggling with mental illnesses. The book shares different stories of people with PTSD from all walks of life.

The power of this book lies in the ability of the people who share their stories so openly. Their personal tragedies, grief, struggles, and recoveries are relatable. As they lay bare their souls to us, we the readers see ourselves and subsequently find ways that we can begin to see "the light" in our lives too.

Brian said it best when he wrote there is no manual to life. I would add, nor is there a specific manual for recovery. As we are all impacted by events differently, each of us has a unique path to recovery. It's not a one-size-fits-all approach. Through their humility in sharing their stories, they provide us several gifts. They help us recognize we can all be vulnerable at one time or another. They demonstrate that these vulnerabilities are not abnormal or anything to be ashamed of, but rather something that is to be acknowledged and addressed. Lastly and most importantly, they give us all hope.

We *are* all in this together, and even in dark times, there is still light in the darkness. Enjoy and Godspeed.

—Thor Eells, Executive Director, National Tactical
  Officers Association

PREFACE

Lord, we pray for the power to be gentle,
the strength to be forgiving;
the patience to be understanding;
and the endurance to accept the consequences of
holding to what we believe is right.
May we put our trust in the power of good to overcome evil and
the power of love to overcome hatred. We pray for the vision to
see and the faith to believe in a world emancipated from violence,
a new world where fear shall no longer lead men to commit
injustice, nor selfishness make them bring suffering to others.
Help us to devote our whole life and thought and
energy to the task of making peace,
praying always for the inspiration and the power
to fulfill the destiny for which we
and all men were created.

—Week of Prayer and World Peace, 1978

It took more than three years to film and edit our international award-winning documentary, *Light in the Darkness: Living Well After Trauma*. We spent much of that time interviewing survivors of different types of traumatic experiences. We also talked to therapists, researchers, and healers to provide insight into approaches to living through and beyond the sometimes lifelong consequences of trauma, including post-traumatic stress disorder (PTSD). During the premiere of our seventy-five-minute film in Green Bay, Wisconsin, audience reactions included laughter and tears. That was our intent—there are so many facets to acknowledging and processing through trauma.

At the premiere, people asked whether we had plans to do something more, perhaps offer a toolbox of resources or even more relatable stories. Our audience understood that trauma does not discriminate against its victims and wanted more education and awareness to complement the film they had just watched. Our audience included psychotherapists, medical doctors, and community leaders who worked directly with clients who have PTSD.

During our mental health panel discussion later that night, it was crystal clear that the audience wanted more understanding of PTSD, trauma, and grief. The panel shared that many people weren't aware of the interventions available or found them too costly to explore. They were ready to take a deeper dive into some of the groundbreaking tools shared in the film. Everyone agreed it was time to lift the stigma of mental illness. Today, the world is finally ready to receive this message.

This book is the result of that request to take a deeper dive. In it, we have included many of the interviews generously given by trauma survivors and healers in the film and our personal stories of trauma and grief. The numerous tools we discovered during the filmmaking process are all in here enhanced by some additional professional guidance.

> It is better to light a candle than to curse the darkness.
>
> –Chinese Proverb

As documentary filmmakers, we submit our films to independent film festivals that are critiqued by peers in the film industry on the efficacy of message and cinematic expression. These festivals provide us exposure on a local, national, or global scale. At the Sundance or Tribeca Film Festivals we compete with over ten thousand other submissions. It's intense. We received over 20 nominations and a healthcare awareness award for our film *Light in the Darkness* prior to its nationwide release. We won Best Documentary in multiple countries and a healthcare award.

In late March 2020, three months before *Light in the Darkness* was to debut nationwide, something happened that none of us could have predicted. The pandemic and subsequent quarantine forced us to cancel all film screenings across the country. It was a huge, unexpected setback;

however, nothing could have prepared us for what happened next.

Already feeling the pressure of the unknown, I, Kimberly, lost my youngest son, Taylor, age fifteen, in an accident. Losing a child engenders a chronic, despairing pain, unlike any other. Brian, my best friend; business partner, and co-author of this book, was with me when we learned what happened.

Taylor's death turned our world upside down, to say the least. It was tempting to put this book idea on a shelf and bury ourselves in grief privately. We believe everyone would have understood. Instead, we internalized it and made the conscious decision to share our story openly in PART II Grief: Unfoldment of the Plan. We recognize that sharing the devastating story of Taylor's death, while painful, has been essential to our healing thus far and is also associated with PTSD.

There is no one way to recover and heal from any trauma. Each survivor chooses their own path or stumbles across it.

−Laurie Matthew, *Behind Enemy Lines*

Healing One Day at a Time

We recognize how prevalent PTSD is within the first responder and military communities. The intention of the book and our documentary is not only to acknowledge and recognize these brave people who have given and suffered much for our communities. It's to acknowledge that we all have life-altering experiences that can be equally as challenging and yet, with help, recovered from.

Both of us have been deeply imprinted by traumatic experiences in our lives and are acutely aware of the association between PTSD and grief. Throughout this book, we will share more about our personal traumas that inspired us to create the documentary and eventually this book. We formed our company, Conscious Content, to give voice to those who need it most, those who are facing the darkest obstacles and struggling to bear their burdens. At Conscious Content, we advocate education and awareness on issues that matter to humanity. As we continue to grow and get healthier ourselves using "out of the box" treatment options for PTSD and grief, we felt others might find value in this as well.

The very tools that we offer in this book are the same ones that are helping us each day on our healing journeys to move through and beyond our PTSD and grief. We also acknowledge we are giving the reader a rare experience of witnessing the processing of grief as it unfolds in "real-time". There is no manual to this life. It unfolds one day at a time. While our book has stories of trauma and life lessons, we balance it with examples of how faith, hope, and action can heal. Ultimately, we believe that you are the curator of your path when it comes to healing from

PTSD, and we encourage you to try out as many offerings in this book as you feel compelled to explore.

> You have the power to hold yourself back or heal
> yourself back together again.
> Ultimately, you make the decision.
>
> –Kimberly Resch

Brian Ross

Having experienced PTSD symptoms for most of my life, I have leaned on my strong relationship with God and my faith to guide and support me on my journey countless times. I have been humbled each time I made it through a circumstance that should have ended my life here on earth. I have had multiple opportunities to pull out a "second chance."

> Don't we all want a second chance? You have an opportunity
> because there's tomorrow. Hope will get you up and get you
> going when everyone and everything drags you down.
>
> –Dr. John King

These near-death experiences have most definitely left an impact on me foundationally. As I reflect on these experiences, I clearly see that each time I survived was a miracle. The feeling of gratitude moves through me as I facilitate my purpose as divinely guided.

Our lives are profound and involve a series of choices. To reach most of humanity with our message, it must resonate on a spiritual level of universal truth. We believe humans are innately good. We encourage others (and ourselves) to have the fortitude to heal the wounds we have acquired along the path. Lifting the stigma has never been a bigger conversation than it is right now. Human beings can be resilient and strong at the same time they are vulnerable and delicate. Let's take this journey together.

Using Wisdom to Get Better

We wrote our book because we wanted people to be aware of PTSD and empowered by the tools we provide to get help now and not push it aside. It's naive to think PTSD will go away or get better on its own without going through the healing process. If you put the work into it, you will be healthier and stronger.

We chose the subtitle for our film, *Living Well After Trauma*, because we feel it's essential to live well. The meaning of the word well is in a good or satisfactory manner. We all have the opportunity to live a good life. That's why we've included "The Wisdom Well" at the end of each chapter. It's a figurative toolbox. We chose this description because we believe this well of wisdom is empowering to the practitioner and reader who is ready to implement one or all of these instruments. All resources in the Wisdom

Well can be accessed on https://Consciouscontent.org by clicking on the Wisdom Well Resources link.

Wisdom takes intelligence a step further. With wisdom, you take what you learn and apply it to your life. That's why each droplet from The Wisdom Well contains a reading, listening/watching, and taking action section with plenty of options to try. It's up to you to choose what path works best for you. We have incorporated Fishing in The Wisdom Well activities throughout the book that you can do in five minutes or less. Rays of Light are sprinkled throughout the book to motivate and inspire you. They are mantras to draw upon in dark moments, perhaps reminders of the progress in healing.

The bottom line is to be proactive, moving forward with your acquired wisdom. Our best defense working through previous trauma is to talk about it, become our own internal advocate for healing ourselves, and spread the word that we can all move through the healing process together and see the light.

At times, you may feel you want to read something, see it visually, etc. Everyone learns differently. Some learn better by hearing; others do better with seeing (reading) while others are encouraged to take action. We've developed each of these areas so you can take a sip of The Wisdom Well in a way that is most comfortable for you.

INTRODUCTION:
Life Interrupted

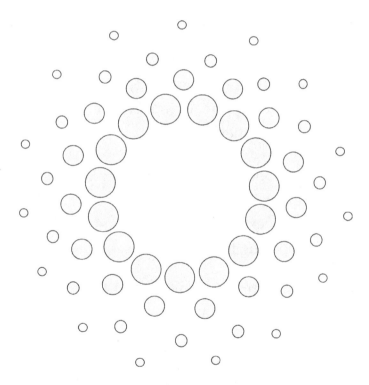

You are a light in the darkness.

-Kimberly Resch and Brian Ross

Planting the PTSD Seed through Childhood Trauma

Brian Ross

Several years ago, I was struggling with how to handle my oldest daughter's anger-filled meltdowns. She was only five years old at the time, and she could put up a significant fight when she didn't get her way, mostly when she was overly tired. One day, while talking to my mom about it, she said, "Brian, do you remember anything before the age of five or six?"

I thought about it for a few seconds and then said, "Actually, no, Mom. I don't really remember any of my early childhood. Why is that?"

"Don't worry about it. You do whatever is necessary to get that child under control while she's young." Her words rang true to my experiences for the first time in decades. They were shocking to hear.

I was born in Fort Lauderdale, Florida, but my parents are from Canada. My dad left a successful family business and moved us down to Florida because he had caught a severe case of pneumonia. He literally lost a rib so the doctors could drain the fluid in his lungs. He needed to live in a warmer climate to survive.

As noted, I don't remember much of my childhood before the age of six. Perhaps that is a good thing because my dad was a pretty intense guy. He was really dominant and reactive toward my older brothers and me. From what I remember, my mom just stayed out of it. I don't think he found the happiness and success he was hoping for once we moved down to Florida. Sometimes it seemed as if he took his insecurities out on my brothers and me physically and emotionally.

Most of the time, the episodes with my dad were just verbal. He'd often yell in a threatening manner about something I did or didn't do well enough. However, on some occasions, they became physical altercations. Some of those would leave marks; on a couple occasions, I recall they required stitches. Every time this happened, it left me feeling small and demeaned.

When I was seven, I brought home a bad progress report with some D's on it, during the last part of second grade. I was struggling to settle into my new environment and a new school. My dad explained he didn't want a bad progress report to turn into a bad report card. His punishment was making me pull down my pants and giving me a spanking just before I left for school each morning for an entire week. I would pull up my pants, grab my books and lunch box, and walk to school with my new neighborhood friends feeling frazzled, scared, and confused by what had just happened. The hope of each new day that week was dismantled by this action each morning. My undeveloped child brain had already moved onto a new moment, and my dad's action would hurl me back into the trauma— this time without context because it was a new day. How did my dad think this was a good idea?

> Healing is like an onion. As you process through one layer of trauma to release the pain and heal, a new layer will surface. One layer after another layer will bring up new issues to focus on. Pace yourself. Only focus on one layer at a time.
>
> —Dana Arcuri,
> *Soul Cry: Releasing & Healing the Wounds of Trauma*

My oldest brother, David, who is almost ten years older than me, moved out at around age eighteen with plans of marriage and a new life. My other brother, Brad, was forced to move out after having a physical altercation with my dad. He defended me after my dad lost his temper and threw me into a door casing and wounded my head, resulting in a few stitches. This left me alone at age nine to deal with my dad with no buffer from my brothers.

By the time I was a young teenager, I struggled with my relationship with my father. It was stressful for me most of the time. He was unpredictable, on edge, and angry.

Unexpectedly, one afternoon when I was at the beach surfing with some friends, my fifty-four-year-old father passed away. Later, we discovered that hemochromatosis, a rare condition in which the body absorbs too much iron, was likely the cause of his untimely death.

Before he died, I remember wishing he would die, so I didn't have to deal with the pain anymore. On this day, he did. I wondered if my thoughts of wishing him dead caused it to happen. This guilt has been a part of my adult narrative. I most likely didn't process the trauma from that day properly. I didn't know how. I wasn't given a manual.

> You are not responsible for anything that happens to you as a child but you are 100% responsible for your own healing.
>
> –Johnnie Dent Jr., Author of *The Anything Every Man*

What I've learned as a father has guided me in the opposite direction as a disciplinarian. I have a much more docile demeanor toward my two daughters. As they grow, I continue to strengthen my communication with my daughters in a protective and serving nature. I am now open to having those tougher conversations when necessary. I have begun to question some of my thinking and actions. I continue to explore what causes or triggers me to do what I do by asking myself questions and searching for answers.

I began to wonder, *What are the implications of family history regarding trauma? Was my daughter's anger somehow connected to my unresolved childhood anger? Is the way I discipline similar to or opposite of my father because of experience or genetics? Who was running the programs? My DNA or my mind?*

Intergenerational Trauma and How It Impacts Future Generations

In the mid to late 2000s, when Brent Bezo, a doctoral psychology student at Carleton University in Ottawa, Canada, and his wife were living in Ukraine, he began noticing a subtle kind of social hostility and mistrust among the population. While conversing with his neighbors, he heard references to the Holodomor, the mass starvation of millions of Soviet Ukrainians that happened from 1932 to 1933. It is considered by many to be an intentional genocide orchestrated by Joseph Stalin's regime.

Could something like this that happened seventy-five years ago still be haunting these people? To find out, he conducted a pilot study of forty-five people from three generations of fifteen Ukrainian families: those who had lived through the Holodomor, their children, and their grandchildren. He discovered that all forty-five people had risky health behaviors, anxiety and shame, food hoarding, overeating, authoritarian parenting styles, high emotional neediness on the part of parents, and low community trust and cohesiveness—what many would describe as living in "survival mode."[1]

Each generation passed on to their children what they had learned from the previous generation, such as not trusting others. He is now conducting a larger study to compare intergenerational effects among Ukrainians who remained in the country after the Holodomor, those who emigrated, and a group of Ukrainians unaffected by the event. The work is part of an emerging line of research that explores whether and how mass cultural and historical traumas affect future generations. The transgenerational effects are not only psychological, but familial, social, cultural, neurobiological, and possibly even genetic.[2]

How We Carry Oppression Through the Generations

Intergenerational trauma isn't talked about a lot unless you see a mental health professional who happens to ask about it. Trauma therapists recognize the importance of addressing this when it comes to intergenerational problems such as oppression that might result from trauma like rape or sexual abuse.

Licensed therapist Támara Hill wrote a blog about intergenerational trauma and how it affects families. She shared,

"A mother who is struggling with her daughter's sexual abuse might also have been sexually abused by her father, who may have also been sexually abused by his father. The impact of generational trauma is significant. A parent or grandparent who never truly healed from or explored their own trauma may find it very difficult to provide emotional support to a family member suffering from his or her own trauma."[3]

Hill's example of intergenerational trauma and the focus of Gardener's services parallel themes in transgenerational programming discussed by Patrick Obissier, a biological decoding therapist specializing in biogenealogy and the psychic roots of illness, both of which can pave the way to freedom from ancestral origins of disease. Obissier has studied a variety of holistic therapies to discern the role trauma and disease play in humans, society, the environment, and the psycho-cerebro-physical effects that manifest in the human body. His book, *Biogenealogy: Decoding the Psychic Roots of Illness*, specifically addresses transgenerational programming in chapter 14. In his book, Obissier examines the question, "To what extent are psychological, traumatic, and survival experiences of our ancestors passed to us through our DNA and to what extent must we consider transgenerational transmission of trauma and disease in our search for healing?"[4] Compelling examples supporting his ideas are woven throughout his book grounded in the principles of biological decoding.

When there is a traumatic unexpected event, with no immediate solution, and it cannot be expressed, the body downloads the trauma into an organ or gland, which then has the assignment to resolve the trauma. The body resolves this biologically as creating a tumor, ulcer, or stop of a specific organ or endocrine function. That is biological decoding.

—Kari Uselman, Ph.D.

Biological Decoding

Kari Uselman, Ph.D., is nationally certified in Biofeedback and Complex Homeopathy and is the founder of Wellness Essentials, LLC, in Oshkosh, Wisconsin. Kari holds a doctorate in Wellness and Education and specializes in holistic wellness. Kari explains that biological decoding is an evolving science supporting a paradigm shift in understanding and treating trauma, illness, disease, and recovery. This rich, growing body of research explores the effects of trauma on human physiology, offering a missing piece to healing.[5] It works for those who are ready to explore and reframe a traumatic experience. This modality cannot be forced, only embraced with certainty and love to be effective.[6]

Trauma begins with a shock, a precise event at an exact time. Things may be going well, and suddenly something traumatic happens. There is a before, and there is an after. The traumatic event enters into the biology with the following criteria: an unexpected, sudden, extreme shock; no immediate solution; and the subsequent unexpressed emotional isolation.[7] At that moment, the trauma unconsciously enters the body. The event becomes a biological, felt sensation that imprints as a bull's-eye in the brain, ushering in PTSD. The bull's-eye spots in the brain disrupt neuro-communication. The longer the traumatic event goes unresolved, the more our biology is stressed.

When a solution such as the passing of time or psychotherapy, neurolinguistic programming, somato-emotional release, or other cellular release therapy presents and the trauma is reframed, the body repairs and the spots in the brain disappear. This is where fungus, viruses, and bacteria play a positive role in regaining emotional balance and can be reframed as helpers. In this model, microbes become the messengers when the neural-networks short circuit due to a shocking trauma. Microbes are the cellular solution to restoring biologized conflicts so that the body can reboot and restore. Fungi cleanse the body of excess matter, bacteria sweep away debris and restore cells, and viruses reconstruct new tissue—a reframe with vast and fascinating implications.[8]

This comprehensive and growing scientific field is rooted in the controversial life work of Dr. Ryke Hamer, a German oncologist. Dr. Hamer's research in the 1970s mapped thousands of traumatic conflicts represented by bull's-eye rings in brain CAT scans. Hamer correlated specific bull's-eye spots in the brain to specific diseases and emotional conflicts, laying the foundation of the New German Medicine.[9] Hamer's research has been added to and expanded over the past five decades by visionary scientists and therapists, including psychiatrist Claude Sabbah, psychotherapist Christian Fleche, therapist Patrick Obissier, and Enrique Boron, a biological decoding educator. The research in this field examines mind-body connection, identifying and consciously addressing emotional traumas or shocks that lead to physical stress and disease.

When the core traumatic unresolved event is decoded and supported with the right psycho, semato, and neuro-linguistic techniques, the body can heal.[10] It takes consciousness and courage to look back and map pivotal life events. Sometimes there is a theme within yourself or your genealogy. When we break the isolation, we can begin to heal with the right support.

How Our Bodies Hold onto Childhood Trauma

As humans, we are exposed to more traumatizing events than you might think. Kaiser Permanente and the Centers for Disease Control and Prevention (CDC) conducted a study from 1995 to 1997, where they discovered that two-thirds of the 17,000 participants suffered from some trauma or adverse childhood experience (ACE). The study findings suggest ACEs are major risk factors for the leading causes of illness, disability, and death in the United States.

According to the Adverse Childhood Experiences Study, the rougher your childhood, the higher your score is likely to be and the higher your risk for later health problems. The study's results suggest that maltreatment and household dysfunction in childhood contribute to health problems decades later. These include chronic diseases—such as heart disease, cancer, stroke, and diabetes—that are the most common causes of death and disability in the United States.[11]

Surprisingly, this study didn't receive a lot of press until it went viral in 2014 when pediatrician Dr. Nadine Burke Harris did a TEDMED Talk on how childhood trauma affects health across a lifetime. Her entire health-care practice is built around trauma.

Experience has taught us that we have only one enduring weapon in our struggle against mental illness: the emotional discovery and emotional acceptance of the truth in the individual and unique history of our childhood.

— Alice Miller, *The Drama of the Gifted Child: The Search for the True Self*

Consider Taking This Short Quiz

Curious about how you might score on the ACES Test? Take a few minutes to complete this original test developed by the CDC:[12]

Prior to your 18th birthday:

Did a parent or other adult in the household often or very often . . . Swear at you, insult you, put you down, or humiliate you? Or act in a way that made you afraid that you might be physically hurt?

No___ If Yes, enter 1 ___

Did a parent or other adult in the household often or very often . . . Push, grab, slap, or throw something at you? Or ever hit you so hard that you had marks or were injured?

No___ If Yes, enter 1 ___

Did an adult or person at least 5 years older than you ever . . . Touch or fondle you or have you touch their body in a sexual way? Or attempt or actually have oral, anal, or vaginal intercourse with you?

No___ If Yes, enter 1 ___

Did you often or very often feel that . . . No one in your family loved you or thought you were important or special? Or, your family didn't look out for each other, feel close to each other, or support each other?

No___ If Yes, enter 1 ___

Did you often or very often feel that . . . You didn't have enough to eat, had to wear dirty clothes, and had no one to protect you? Or your parents were too drunk or high to take care of you or take you to the doctor if you needed it?

No___ If Yes, enter 1 ___

Were your parents ever separated or divorced?

No___ If Yes, enter 1 ___

Was your mother or stepmother:

Often or very often pushed, grabbed, slapped, or had something thrown at her? Or sometimes, often, or very often kicked, bitten, hit with a fist, or hit with something hard? Or ever repeatedly hit over at least a few minutes or threatened with a gun or knife?

No___ If Yes, enter 1 ___

Did you live with anyone who was a problem drinker or alcoholic, or who used street drugs?

No___ If Yes, enter 1 ___

Was a household member depressed or mentally ill, or did a household member attempt suicide?

No___ If Yes, enter 1 ___

Did a household member go to prison?

No___ If Yes, enter 1 ___

Now add up your "Yes" answers: ___ This is your ACE Score

What does your score mean?

As your ACE score increases, so does the risk of disease, social, and emotional problems. With an ACE score of 4 or more, things start getting serious. The likelihood of chronic pulmonary lung disease increases 390 percent; hepatitis, 240 percent; depression 460 percent; attempted suicide, 1,220 percent.[13]

The Mind-Body Connection

Throughout her career, Candace Pert, Ph.D., conducted pioneering research on the connection between our minds and bodies. In her groundbreaking book, *Molecules of Emotion: The Science Behind Mind-Body Medicine*, she answers questions that have perplexed scientists and healers for years:

Why do we feel the way we feel?

How do our thoughts and emotions affect our health?

Are our bodies and minds distinct from one another, or do they function as parts of an interconnected system?

This book explores holistic treatment modalities to help heal through trauma. While we respect Western allopathic medicine, we believe these effective alternatives have merit and deserve recognition. That's why we've interviewed healing practitioners, and we back up what they say with science.

Most psychologists treat the mind as disembodied, a phenomenon with little or no connection to the physical body. Conversely, physicians treat the body with no regard to the mind or the emotions. But the body and mind are not separate, and we cannot treat one without the other.

— Candace Pert, Ph.D., Neuroscientist,
Author of *Molecules of Emotion:
The Science Behind Mind-Body Medicine*[14]

Note all the resources listed here can be accessed on https://Consciouscontent.org by clicking on the Wisdom Well Resources link.

THE WISDOM WELL

Reading:

What Are the Differences Between PTS and PTSD? Post-traumatic stress (PTS) is not considered a mental disorder while PTSD is considered a clinically diagnosable disorder usually requiring professional help. PTS symptoms are common after a traumatic event and may improve or resolve within a month. PTSD symptoms are more severe, persistent, can interfere with daily functioning, and can last for more than a month.

Post Traumatic Stress , Confusion and Anger: How Quarantine Affects Your Mental Health. Life in quarantine can negatively affect your mental health, causing post-traumatic stress, confusion and even anger, a study from King's College London shows. But by getting uncensored access to up-to-date information, staying in touch with loved ones, and keeping active on social media, researchers believe these negative effects can be staved off.

Obissier, Patrick. *Biogenealogy: Decoding the Psychic Roots of Illness.* Rochester, VT. Healing Arts Press, 2006. Reveals the psychic causes of illness and how to decode and resolve them. Explains how we inherit illness from our ancestors via cellular memory and provides protocols for diagnosis and treatment. Demonstrates how illness is an ally that enables individuals to restore balance to both their life and that of their family tree.

Flèche, Christian. *The Biogenealogy Sourcebook: Healing the Body by Resolving Traumas of the Past.* Rochester, VT. Healing Arts Press, 2008. A practical guide to the correspondence between emotion, organ systems, and disease. Identifies what emotional shocks will engender illnesses specific to a certain part of the body. Shows how illness is an ally that enables individuals to restore balance to their health.

Martel, Jacques. *The Complete Dictionary of Ailments and Diseases.* Charlsbourg (QC) Canada: Les Editions ATMA Internationals, New Leaf Distributing Company, 2012. The most comprehensive dictionary dealing with the conflicted thoughts, feelings, and emotions at the root of illnesses.

Watching/Listening:

"What Parts of the Brain Are Impacted by PTSD?" (1:07) From the frontal lobe (which houses our emotions) to the amygdala (which oversees our fight or flight response), Michael Roy, MD, Col. (Ret.) explains how parts of the brain are affected when injured by a traumatic experience, whether physical, emotional, or both.

"How Childhood Trauma Affects Health Across a Lifetime." (15:51) Childhood trauma isn't something you just get over as you grow up. In this TEDx Talk, pediatrician Nadine Burke Harris explains how the repeated stress of abuse, neglect, and parents struggling with mental health or substance abuse issues has real, tangible effects on brain development.

"A Quick and Simple Way to Think About the Brain." (2:38) The brain is a complex system made up of three vital layers. Having even one dysfunctional layer can cause fear, frustration, and heartache. Get a deeper understanding on how the brain works in this short video.

Taking Action:

Visit https://Consciouscontent.org to see why we are humanity's media company and find all kinds of mental health resources. You can also view behind the scenes footage of our film with exclusive interviews from survivors.

Subscribe to Conscious Content Collective on YouTube, where our mission is to be Humanity's Media Company. Our videos will inspire you and get you thinking.

Visit The German/Germanic New Medicine, which offers medical verification of Dr. Ryke's biological decoding research. Dr. Ryke's work was highly criticized when introduced to mainstream medicine in the 1970s resulting in the removal of his medical license. His research has since been verified by many.

PART I

Experiences: Living with PTSD

Bad things do happen, how I respond to them defines my character and the quality of my life. I can choose to sit in perpetual sadness, immobilized by the gravity of my loss, or I can choose to rise from the pain and treasure the most precious gift I have – life itself.

–Walter Anderson, American playwright

Post-traumatic stress disorder (PTSD) can occur when people experience extremely traumatic events, such as combat crime, an accident, or natural disaster. While it doesn't matter how you got the trauma, the feeling of "catching" PTSD remains the same (even if you don't know you have it). Intrusive memories, flashbacks, and nightmares may occur as you relive the event over and over again in your mind. Consider it "life interrupted."

In this chapter, you'll read the stories of many different people who have PTSD. While we all come from different backgrounds and have unique stories to share, PTSD is our common denominator. In April 2018, the Ruderman Family Foundation conducted a study where they found that police officers and firefighters are more likely to die by suicide than in the line of duty. In 2017, at least 103 firefighters and 140 police officers committed suicide. In contrast, 93 firefighters and 129 police officers died in the line of duty.[15] We'll begin by learning more about the dangers of PTSD and first responders.

Post-Traumatic Stress Disorder (PTSD)

According to the National Institute of Mental Health, post-traumatic stress disorder (PTSD) is a disorder that develops in some people who have experienced a shocking, scary, or dangerous event. While it is normal to be afraid during and after a traumatic situation, most people naturally recover from the short-term symptoms. PTSD can occur when the symptoms stick around and become chronic, people can feel stressed, anxiety stricken, or frightened even when they aren't in danger.[16]

To be diagnosed with PTSD, an adult must have all of the following symptoms for at least one month:

1. **Re-experiencing symptoms** (at least one) – These include flashbacks where you relive the trauma over and over again and have physical symptoms like sweating, a racing heart, nightmares, or frightening thoughts. Words, objects, or situations that serve as reminders of the event can also be triggering. Re-experiencing symptoms may disrupt your everyday routine.

2. **Avoidance symptoms** (at least one) – Staying away from places, events, or objects that remind you of the traumatic experience. These symptoms can cause you to change your personal routine.

3

3. **Arousal and reactivity symptoms** (at least two) – Includes being easily startled, feeling tense or "on edge", difficulty sleeping, and angry outbursts. Arousal symptoms are usually constant, instead of being triggered by things that remind you of the traumatic events. These symptoms can make you feel stressed and angry making it hard to do daily tasks, such as sleeping, eating, or concentrating.

4. **Cognition and mood symptoms** (at least two) – This includes having angry outbursts, trouble remembering key features of the traumatic event, negative thoughts about yourself or the world, distorted feelings like guilt or blame, and loss of interest in enjoyable activities. These symptoms can begin or worsen after the traumatic event but are not due to injury or substance use. These symptoms can make you feel alienated or detached from friends or family members.

It is natural to have some of these symptoms for a few weeks after a dangerous event. When the symptoms last more than a month, seriously affect one's ability to function, and are not due to substance use, medical illness, or anything except the event itself, they might be PTSD. Some people with PTSD don't show any symptoms for weeks or months. Depression, substance abuse, or one or more of the other anxiety disorders often accompany PTSD.[17]

PTSD can occur at any age. "Fight-or-flight" biological instincts, which can be life-saving during a crisis, can leave us with ongoing symptoms. Because the body is busy increasing its heart rate, pumping blood to muscles, preparing the body to fight or flee, all our physical resources and energy are focused on getting out of harm's way. Therefore, there has been discussion that the posttraumatic stress response may not be an actual disorder, but rather a variant of a human response to trauma. According to the U.S. Department of Veterans Affairs,

> An estimated 8 out of every 100 people (and growing) will experience PTSD in their lifetime

> Women have a higher rate than men (10% compared to 4%) due to sexual assault, however, hormones can also play a part in the increased percentage

> Out of 24 countries studied, the US ranked 4th behind Canada, The Netherlands, and Australia[18]

According to Canada's National Centre for PTSD, a 2020 survey on trauma based on 24 countries noted that most trauma originates from the following:

Sexual violence 33%

Interpersonal trauma (death, life threatening illness or trauma of a loved one) 30%

Interpersonal violence (child abuse, violence in the home, physical assault or the threat of violence) 12%

Organized violence exposure (refugees, kidnapping, war zone civilians) 3%

Organized violence participation (witnessing death, injury, finding a dead body, causing injury or death either accidentally or purposefully) 11%

Other traumatic events (vehicle accidents, natural disasters, or being exposed to toxic chemicals) 12%[19]

PTSD symptoms usually begin within three months after experiencing or being exposed to a traumatic event. Occasionally, symptoms may emerge years afterward. For a diagnosis of PTSD, symptoms must last more than one month. Symptoms of depression, anxiety, or substance use often accompany PTSD.

Someone with PTSD may have additional disorders, as well as thoughts of or attempts at suicide:

Anxiety Disorders

Obsessive-Compulsive Disorder (OCD)

Borderline Personality Disorder

Depression

Substance use disorders/Dual Diagnosis

These other illnesses can make it challenging to treat PTSD. For example, medications used to treat OCD or depression may worsen symptoms of PTSD. Successfully treating PTSD almost always improves these related illnesses and successful treatment of depression, anxiety or substance use usually improves PTSD symptoms.[20]

First Responders

We believe first responders—law enforcement personnel, firefighters, emergency medical services (EMS) workers, the military, and anyone who shows up at the scene of an incident first—are seemingly called to their career with a deep devotion to help others in need. They are a unique breed of humans.

This type of selfless service can cause mental, emotional, and physical damage, as it often puts people in harm's way. First responders are usually the first on the scene to challenging, dangerous and draining situations. Many witness horrific scenes often, even daily. Continuous exposure to death and destruction takes a psychological toll that can result in PTSD, substance abuse, depression, and suicide.

First responders must balance being exposed to trauma with taking care of all facets of their health—body, mind, and spirit. As a culture, this group is beginning to acknowledge self-care as the foundational factor to staying healthy in general. The Substance Abuse and Mental Health Services Association (SAMHSA) continues to research treatment modalities to address trauma, including those for first responders.

Here we offer three stories of first responders diagnosed with PTSD because of events that took place while they were doing their job.

Ray Norton, First Responder

The job of a first responder itself is stressful, even though we as first responders don't think it's stressful. The abnormalities that we deal with every day are common for us, but those things add up cumulatively. I did twenty-five years on Bayflite, which is the local air and medical helicopter. We got to see a pretty high acuity of shootings, stabbings. This is the other side of life where people aren't so good. There were a lot of traumatic injuries. It never bothered me, or at least I didn't think so. It's an amazing career, but balancing the stress and everyday life can be a challenge for some.

One of my best friends started in the fire service with me. He took his life, and I found him. He did it in a rather graphic way. That one bothered me. That one bothered me a lot, and I didn't realize how much, but I started having a lot more anger issues and sleep disturbances. I didn't know much about PTSD. It wasn't until I started working with combat vets that I started hearing their stories, and the more I listened to them, the more I realized, "That's me. That's me." The short temper, the anger. I had bad dreams, but I never remembered having bad dreams. I would wake up soaked in sweat or feeling stressed, jaws clenched, never really remembering what the dreams were.

A lot of us just don't know. I think we're so immersed in it every day that we're working in that environment. I don't think a lot of times we stop and think about it. Then when people are having struggles, they are afraid to bring it up because if they bring it up, they are afraid it's going to affect their careers. PTSD in the fire service has not gotten the attention and the focus that it has in the military and veteran populations.[21]

Develop a witness state. You are larger than fear. You are larger than anxiety. When you notice yourself feeling stressed or overwhelmed, tell yourself: "I am not this emotion. I can center myself. I can lovingly detach from my state of overwhelm and lovingly witness the feelings I'm experiencing. Realizing you are larger than the feeling will relax you and offer perspective.

Mike Vaessen, Army Reserves

I was an army officer and major and took three tours overseas to Afghanistan. After my last tour, my friends told me that I changed. My first tour I was an executive officer doing logistics for a military hospital, a Jordanian military hospital, with Afghan interpreters, Afghan citizens coming in every day for medical treatment, some horrible cases. In the United States, you would be in the ICU for weeks and months, but there, it's you're in, you're out. You're in a high-stress day-to-day environment with no days off. You'd be rolling with three, four hours of sleep.

It was definitely cumulative. I wasn't a door-kicker. I didn't get shot. I was logistics and civil affairs, but I saw kids that were burned accidentally, and their skin was just falling off. And there's nothing you can do, you just walk on by. The next day it's something else. Every day is some big spike. If you'd asked me twenty years ago, Could you ever get PTSD? I'd say, "That's just all in your head."

I came home from a tour more closed off, reserved. I really didn't want to do much. I wasn't that active. I didn't want to go out. I'd get the phone calls and ignore them. Just really withdrew. Coworkers found me more aloof. I was nervous in normal situations, meetings. I've had dreams where I thought I was back there. I remember swerving across the highway when I saw a cardboard box because I thought it was an IED [improvised explosive device].[22]

Mental pain is less dramatic than physical pain, but it is more common and also more hard to bear. The frequent attempt to conceal mental pain increases the burden: it is easier to say "My tooth is aching" than to say "My heart is broken."

— C. S. Lewis, *The Problem of Pain*

Tony Seahorn, Army Officer and Combat Veteran

I served in Vietnam as a young twenty-one-year-old army first lieutenant with the First Infantry Division, Black Lions. My primary focus was on the mission and trying to make sure men under my command survived the mission, survived the war, and were ultimately able to return home. When I was in Vietnam, I never spent much time thinking about my own fear, my own vulnerability because I was dedicated to ensuring the strategic operation was carried out as planned.

A year or so after Vietnam, when I was in the hospital recovering from the physical wounds of war, I began to have vivid flashbacks of the horror of combat. I had shrapnel wounds in the chest and bullet damage to my right shoulder and upper arm. A contusion developed on my right arm due to a tourniquet that stopped blood flow for twelve hours during the heat of battle. Initially, the military medical team had planned to amputate my arm to prevent the spread of gangrene to save my life. Through an army nurse's relentless physical therapy, my arm began to show signs of life and my arm was spared. While my attention continued on recovering from the physical wounds of war, the injury I had no control over was what happened in my mind when I was sleeping.

One night I woke up sweating profusely and anxious. I know now I was having a panic attack. I thought I was losing my mind. That was the first onset of PTSD for me. And for the longest time, no one could put a handle on it. If you go back to World War II, they didn't refer to it as PTSD. They called it shell shock or combat fatigue or soldiers' heart. The initial belief was the feeling would eventually go away. Most soldiers would try to suppress the emotional devastation and get on with their lives. My dad served during the Normandy invasion. He had PTSD his entire life, and until Janet and I wrote our book [*Tears of a Warrior*] I never knew what was wrong with my dad, or why he was so cranky, or why he would go off by himself so often. We just thought he didn't love us. I didn't realize that he had PTSD ever since he was nineteen years old in World War II.

I considered myself a relatively strong-minded person who believed that if I could heal from the physical wounds of war, I would be okay. Unfortunately, once I started having nightmares and panic attacks, the more I resisted the feeling, and the more I tried to handle it on my own, the worse it got. It's kind of like the tougher you are, the worse it gets because the wounds are emotional. You're used to handling physical pain but have little or no experience with mental injury. Virtually everyone I talked to about it, including civilian and military psychologists, said, "You'll get over it with time. Don't worry about it." So, for thirty years, I suffered from PTSD.

I would immerse myself in my corporate career. I had a position in management with AT&T. I just worked on projects and focused on other people's problems. Whether it was work problems or home problems, I always focused outside of myself. It wasn't until I came home and tried to decompress that the demons would appear. I had a pretty short fuse sometimes with our sons. Overall, our family life was good. We did everything with the kids; we enjoyed being together and went camping, skiing, hiking, and fishing. The kids loved it, and they traveled with us everywhere. But what I learned and I didn't understand at the time, you can be a good dad for 90 percent of the time, but if you're a crappy dad for 10 percent of the time, the 90 percent doesn't count.

If I'd have a little too much to drink, I'd get kind of gnarly and my emotions would come out. I would say things. I would be real short with my wife, my kids, and some of my dear friends. PTSD took me on an emotional roller coaster for thirty years.

I got drafted into the army as Uncle Sam found out I wasn't in college any longer. Back in those days, you immediately got drafted if you didn't have a recognized deferment. After my basic and advanced army training, I qualified for Officer Candidate School and eventually graduated as a new second lieutenant. Then I attended the Officer Career Program and also qualified for aviation training. Eventually following extensive training and certification, I received orders for deployment to Vietnam with a double MOS [military occupational specialty]. Once in the country, I tried to get into an aviation unit but instead was assigned as the battalion combat communications officer for the Big Red One Black Lions. The Black Lions were a highly respected combat-ready infantry battalion that was noted for pursuing and engaging in combat with the enemy. Most of my Vietnam tour of duty was spent on combat missions.

During one of my more routine flights, I was on a courier mission, and we received a call from troops in distress on the ground. We immediately responded and flew down and loaded some wounded onboard. I got out of my helicopter, helped load the troops, and then just as we began to lift off the enemy came out of the jungle at about 50 yards with small arms fire and RPGs [rocket-propelled grenades]. The copilot lifted the helicopter as I was still standing on to the skid on the outside. We got about treetop level and we took a direct hit from an RPG. The chopper went down. I wasn't belted in yet, so I was thrown from the helicopter when it hit the ground, then it exploded. I was blown free upon impact and landed on my head and neck about 20 yards away. In shock and disbelief, I watched helplessly as everyone on board perished in that helicopter crash. Almost simultaneously, a squad of Cobras and Huey Gunships arrived at the scene and secured the area. I, along with the remaining members of the infantry patrol, were evacuated to safety. Eleven months into my tour as the devastation of war continued, I was severely wounded when a superior enemy force overran our ground NDP [night defensive position]. My tour in Vietnam was over. But little did I know about the challenges ahead. War is hell.

When you're sending people to war, you don't tend to think about PTSD. You send them to war to fight for the cause. The military wants them focused on what they were trained for and what their mission is, not so much about the aftermath of war and experiences that could result in an injury that could be PTSD.

If you look at who was deployed in the Gulf War, Iraq, and now Afghanistan, a lot of those individuals are National Guard on multiple deployments. Which simply says they go out, they serve, they come back home, and supposedly lead a normal life doing their civilian occupation until they're called up again. And so many of them are in this roller-coaster ride of "I'm a warrior today, tomorrow I'm back at home working, and everything's supposed to be normal, and then I'm off to war again."

We used to call it reintegration syndrome. But we now refer to it as moral injury. That phenomenon has been causing a lot of problems, and it's kind of exacerbated the issue of PTSD. Now we're realizing that moral injury is causing a lot of the high suicide rates because people are coming back, they can't adjust, and they can't process what they've seen, experienced, or what they've been around, and they are really struggling.

Often when you go into a third-world country, there are a lot of the things that occur there. Some cultures place a different value on life. Some of their traditions may be unacceptable based on our standards, or their punishment system may appear barbaric and much different than ours. Also, collateral damage—all the innocent people who are impacted by war—can take a tremendous toll on our ability to distinguish right from wrong. We know statistically, that innocent civilians are often the victims of war and can suffer greater mortality than the warriors themselves. So, that's a problem very difficult to process.[23]

> I can tell you as a veteran, if you're missing an arm and a leg, someone thinks you're disabled. But if you are missing something between your ears or in your heart, they can't see it. Therefore, they tend to dismiss it.
>
> — Tony Seahorn

Buried Childhood Sexual Trauma

Childhood sexual abuse is a significant but preventable public health problem. Childhood sexual abuse refers to the involvement of a child (person less than 18 years old) in sexual activity that violates the laws or social taboos of society and that he/she:

does not fully comprehend

does not consent to or is unable to give informed consent to, or

is not developmentally prepared for and cannot give consent to[24]

Although estimates vary across studies, the data shows about one in four girls and one in thirteen boys experience child sexual abuse at some point in childhood. Ninety-one percent of child sexual abuse is perpetrated by someone the child or child's family knows.[25]

Dr. John King, PTSD Survivor: The Flashback

Every springtime I'd walk from my parents' house to school, and there was one lady who grew daffodils. Every year I would look forward to those daffodils sprouting because I thought, "I've made it one more year, and in all the mess that is my life, this is beautiful." I loved those daffodils. I'd smell them. I'd never pick them, because they're just perfect, the big trumpet yellow ones.

It was a Thursday afternoon at about three o'clock. I remember very clearly walking up thinking, "Man, what a beautiful day." I looked out at the daffodils and saw their beauty. At that moment, everything came back. I don't know why that was a trigger, but somehow that was the thing that brought it all back.

Everything came flooding back. It was like my brain decided that I'd suppressed it for thirty-odd years. It was just time to deal with this. I'd go to bed and I'd have nightmares about it. I'd get up, I'd be in business meetings, and it'd be playing before my eyes like a movie screen. It was constantly this barrage of images and thoughts. It was really hard to distinguish between reality and not reality, being awake and asleep.

I went from being a self-confident, outgoing, extroverted person to now pretty much overnight being paranoid, fearful, just concerned for my own safety, and concerned for my kids. I still find crowds difficult. I find new people difficult. I can't trust anyone. That's the voice, you can't trust anyone, you've got to be on your guard. Who's going to hurt you? Are they going to hurt you? Are they going to hurt your kids? Are they going to hurt your wife? I'm on all the time. I'm on when I go out. I'm on when I wake up. I'm on when I'm sitting at home. Even if all the doors are locked, I'm on, just in case someone turns up and wants to hurt me.

What happened to me as a kid? It was a series of sexual situations, being taken to parties and being around pornography and being involved in filming situations and being encouraged to engage in sexual activities with other people. Apparently, I was a good-looking kid, so I was peddled out that way. I recalled the events in 2008. I'd suppressed it up until that point. It was literally like a total personality change. I went from knowing very much who I was and where I was going, operating businesses, flying around the world, doing a whole range of different things, to just, "No, I don't want to do that anymore." I can't do that anymore. I went from being able to speak in front of crowds of 10,000 or 15,000 people to having a chronic stutter and not being able to talk to people and getting panic attacks when I stepped into an elevator.

It cost me my first marriage and estrangement from all my kids for a while there. I'm still estranged from one of them. It's very difficult. I think when you're married to someone for so long and they're a certain way, you come to expect certain things. Now that person who used to go out every day and work and travel and do all that is just sitting in their shed, crying or just not coping or having panic attacks or rage attacks at the oddest things. That's a massive spread for anyone, be it adult or child, to get their head around.

At the time when the recall happened, I was running a church. It was growing. It was prospering. A whole range of things were positive. I explained to a small group of people the challenge I was having with post-traumatic stress. They automatically jumped to conclusions, and because of the stigma attached to mental illness, they just judged me. They just cast aspersions and judgment, came to conclusions about what I would do, what I wouldn't do, what I wasn't able to cope with. I think they stopped seeing me. They stopped seeing me trying. They saw a broken person, which wasn't necessarily the case, but if you're told that all the time, then they come to believe that, because I think people have a difficulty processing this.[26]

Trauma and School Shootings

School shootings have become more frequent in the United States. In these cases, the trauma affects more than those who experienced or witnessed the event. The entire student body, all the teachers and staff, families, and communities suffer too.

Dr. Janet Seahorn knows. In addition to living with someone with PTSD, she was directly exposed to trauma when she worked in central administration for Jefferson County Schools in Colorado, the county in which the Columbine High School shooting happened on April 20, 1999. On this date, two senior high school students murdered twelve students and one teacher and shot twenty-one others before committing suicide. Of the twelve students murdered, ten were killed in the school library. At the time, it was the deadliest school shooting in U.S. history.

As a member of the administration, Dr. Seahorn's role was to deal with students and family members after the tragedy. She shared the following with us in a recent interview:

Janet Seahorn, Ph.D.

It took us probably about a half an hour before we really were getting confirmation of what was taking place and that kids were dying and there were a lot of people injured. There was no plan on how to deal with it as something of this scale had never happened before. At the time, Columbine had about 1,200 students, so all of us in administration took about one hundred names of the students and called their homes.

As we talked to the parents or a sibling, we asked, "Did so-and-so come home?" And they would say, "Yeah, we've heard from them," and then we would mark their name off the list. And if they didn't hear from their student, we'd say, "You need to call us back as soon as you hear from them." By eight o'clock that evening, we had not heard back from thirteen of those families and we knew exactly what was happening. Two families that I personally called did not have their student come home that day.

[Those] most traumatized were the students that were in the immediate vicinity of the shooters—in the cafeteria, the library, and some of the classrooms. The ones who were severely injured experienced essentially what it is like being in combat. They're never going to get over that. The teachers at Columbine, our superintendent, and assistant superintendent didn't sleep for three days. I mean, not at all. They had to go into the school and see everything. I don't even know how they were able to do that. A lot of the first responders, firefighters, and members of the police force could not return to work after that day because they had severe PTSD. They had to choose other careers because it was too painful.

One of our female students was shot and they put her in an ambulance. They weren't sure she was going to make it through. During an TV interview, she talked about how, to this day, she has incredible pain throughout her whole body. Every time she sees somebody in a black trench coat walking down the street, she turns around and goes the other way because it is a direct memory of that fear. Her brain recognizes black trench coats as danger.

Every student and family dealt with it differently. Some families and students took a sense of control and ownership that I'm not even sure I could've done at that time. But they were just amazing people, and a lot of them just had faith in a higher source and some inner strength that not everybody's blessed with. You just learn as a human being. You watch other people go through the most horrible days of their lives and see what they do to make a difference and you say, "I choose to be as much as I can like them." I think those are the lessons we get to use and to try to model and live by in our lives as we go forth.[27]

Accidental Trauma:
Brian Ross Shares His Stories

I've come close to death often. Why I've had so many of these experiences is a mystery to me. Although I survived some horrific accidents and mishaps, I did not deal with them appropriately. At the time, it seemed enough to be relieved and grateful that I hadn't died. But PTSD can be insidious. Although I didn't realize it, I filed these experiences incorrectly in my brain and unwittingly carried the stress with me, leaving lasting scars that caused PTSD.

I'll share some of these experiences with you.

Age 17: Motorcycle Madness

It was New Year's Eve, and my friend Jim was coming to pick me up in his little Suzuki Samurai jeep. We had plans to meet up with some friends and ring in the new year together. Instead, he rolls up with his other Suzuki, a GSX-R 1100, which is essentially a racing motorcycle.

Although Jim was a very experienced driver, I was a little unsure if I wanted to hitch a ride on that beast that night. He convinced me that we only had a couple of miles to go, so it was not a big deal. I regretfully hopped on the back of the bike not listening to the voice in my head that said not to go.

I soon found out that Jim was feeling a little crazy that night and said to me, "we have a little time to kill." He tore out of my mom's driveway like a bat out of hell. He was so proud of himself and how well he could handle that bike. Soon we were speeding down a pitch-black, old country backroad, and Jim pointed at the speedometer as we began to approach 165 miles an hour.

I hadn't been consulted on that spontaneous decision, and by this time, I was angry and yelling at him to slow down. No part of this plan was good, and a bad feeling started to come over me.

I remember the feeling of being airborne. As our senses caught up to what was happening, we realized we had literally run out of road. We missed our turn, and we were now on an even older, worn-out partial clay road heading back into the woods. With trees on both sides of this narrow pass, we saw what looked like taillights up ahead. Jim tried to slow down by laying the motorcycle on its side. We slid just before hitting what we later learned was a car going down this same gnarly road.

This car turned out to be our saving grace. We slid into this moving vehicle with a hard crash, but we didn't hit one of those many solid, unyielding trees, which would have killed us instantly. We hit something moving in the same direction as we were, which softened the blow tremendously. The bike was mangled and smoking, yet still miraculously running.

We were bloody and dirty from scraping the road but were wearing helmets and were alive and okay. It was dark and dusty illuminated by only the lights of the vehicle we just struck. The people in the car were not injured, but appeared to be in shock. They said they'd heard us coming down the road and saw our lights before impact. They tried to help us clean up with tissues from their car.

I said to Jim as he sobbed and tried to apologize: "I need you to know that God placed his hand on this car on this old dark road tonight and caught us. There is no other reason we should be standing here alive tonight. One or both of us must have something important to get done in this life."

Ray of Light

I believe all of us have the innate ability to access the knowledge or knowingness that is God. If we ask and listen, we are all offered the answers we need at that moment. Often, today in our noisy world of distractions, it requires more focus but it is still available for all of us. I had a bad feeling about that night. A voice inside me was telling me not to get on the motorcycle. I should have listened. Fortunately, God had plans for me and stepped in and saved me.

Age 18: Missed It by That Much

In high school, I had my second brush with death. I was with my best friend, Nate, and a couple other schoolmates in his car. We were driving home from the mall after picking up our tuxedos for Homecoming. Usually, I'm in the passenger seat, but this time I was in the backseat. We were in a hurry to get home, and it was extremely windy out that day. We got stuck behind a slow car on a two-lane road. Nate was getting frustrated and decided it was time to pass some cars. It turned out that we needed to pass about ten cars to get back into our lane, and a huge semi truck was quickly approaching and coming straight at us.

Nate has a pretty fast car, and as we were passing these cars the wind was blowing so hard he was struggling to stay in the lane. Meanwhile, the semi was barreling down on us while the driver was flashing his lights at us to get over. We were freaking out at this point, but at the very last second, Nate whipped the car back into our lane going about 95 miles an hour.

I believe that the combination of the extremely high winds and Nate having to switch lanes so fast to avoid the truck caused Nate's car to spin like the blades of a helicopter. We narrowly missed a head-on collision with the semi truck but were now spiraling across the centerline and back into oncoming traffic. We managed to avoid colliding with the oncoming cars and left the highway, finally reaching the left grass shoulder of the road. It felt as if we had started to accelerate, maybe because the tires were worn down from spinning and created less friction.

The next thing I saw was this giant pine tree on the other side of the road, and we were heading straight for it. Time seemed to slow down as I watched it get closer and closer. I prayed to God that we wouldn't hit it. Then I realized we were going to hit it. We were going so fast and this tree was getting so big. There was no way to miss it and then bam!

The sound of the car striking that big tree just off center was unlike anything I have ever heard. Nate's car was destroyed, but all four of us were okay. Another blessing.

The force of the impact blasted me out the hatch window. I guess I didn't have a seatbelt on or it was ripped out, but I was holding onto the front seatbelt with my hand. As I shattered the rear window with my back, the passenger side seat belt I was grasping onto prevented me from being thrown out of the car. Of the four of us, I was the only one who ended up going to the hospital, but only for a few stitches in my back.

I couldn't believe I walked away from this one too. The EMTs said we were saved because we didn't hit the tree precisely in the middle of the car, which may have meant certain death for some or all of us that day at that speed. They said someone must be looking out for us. Now I was really beginning to believe that was true.

Ray of Light

Oftentimes in life we feel rushed. We feel like there just isn't enough time to get things done. I have for most of my life felt this way. It creates an unnecessary stress in our lives and in most cases I have found that it's just not true. If we want our lives to be productive, full of joy and fulfillment, I have found that planning your life can really help to eliminate the stressful feeling we put on ourselves when we're feeling stressed about time. A simple list of priorities written down or placed in a calendar can really help a person stay focused in the moment and allow your day to unfold rather than having it take over.

Age 21: Yet Another Brush with Death

I had just received my scuba diving certification with my friend Rodney. We were excited to dive on our own and went to the Blue Springs in Florida, which is approximately 110 feet deep. We were both good swimmers and in good shape but rookie scuba divers. We decided to dive down to a ledge at about 65 feet underwater.

When in deep water, divers can experience something I would describe as feeling a little bit drunk. It's disorienting and can cause divers to have poor judgment and dive even deeper. I was hanging upside down from this underwater ledge watching my bubbles float all the way to the surface through the beautiful sun rays shining down from way above. I was in a deep meditation.

At approximately 65 feet, the bubbles I was blowing got bigger and bigger as they approached the surface because the pressure decreases on the air inside the bubble. It was quite beautiful.

At the same time, my regulator, which provides all this oxygen I have been using from the air tank that was strapped to my back, began to give me a hard time. I'm thinking it is because I have been hanging upside down. Remember, this was my first real dive without an instructor, and I am not 6 feet down in a pool. I blew out another breath as I flipped around right side up and then tried to take a breath in. I pursed my lips together completely and tried to suck air but there wasn't any air to take. I thought, *This is not happening!*

I pulled my gauges into view. I was completely out of air. I had just breathed out my last breath. I had no air in my lungs, and I was 65 feet from the surface—a long way to swim without oxygen. I remembered my instructor telling me, "Whatever you do underwater, never ever panic or you will most likely die."

Rodney was about 10 feet above me. I swam to him and made a slashing gesture across my throat with my hand—the universal scuba signal for "I am out of air." Rodney's eyes just about popped out of his head as we had just learned these hand gestures. Also a novice, he couldn't get to his alternate regulator, so we shared his. Another big no-no. Fortunately even though Rodney and I had been underwater for the same amount of time, he still had some air left but very little.

We realized the only option was for us to take turns breathing and begin our ascent up to the surface. That was a bonding experience. I never loved anyone more in that moment than I loved my friend Rodney. Somehow, we got back up to the surface and were okay.

Consider Taking a Test

After reading through some of these stories, you may wonder whether you suffer from PTSD. Many people don't realize they have PTSD. Being diagnosed can be a relief to many because it explains why they think and behave the way they do. It tells them that they are not crazy. But know that not every person who experiences a traumatic event will be diagnosed with PTSD. Trauma does not always change how the brain is wired.

If you haven't been diagnosed with PTSD and you aren't sure you have it, the following screening measure can help you determine whether you might benefit from professional attention. This screening tool is not designed to make a diagnosis of PTSD but to be shared with your primary care physician or mental health professional to inform further conversations about diagnosis and treatment.

Post-Traumatic Stress Disorder Screening Tool[28]

Are you troubled by the following?

☐ Yes ☐ No   You have experienced or witnessed a life-threatening event.

Do you have intrusions about the event in at least one of the following ways?

☐ Yes ☐ No   Repeated, distressing memories, or dreams

☐ Yes ☐ No   Acting or feeling as if the event were happening again (flashbacks or a sense of reliving it)

❒ Yes ❒ No   Intense physical and/or emotional dis-
                tress when you are exposed to things that
                remind you of the event

Do you avoid things that remind you of the event in at
least one of the following ways?

❒ Yes ❒ No   Avoiding thoughts, feelings, or conversa-
                tions about it
❒ Yes ❒ No   Avoiding activities and places or people
                who remind you of it

Since the event, do you have negative thoughts and
mood associated with the event in at least 2 of the following ways?

❒ Yes ❒ No   Blanking on important parts of it
❒ Yes ❒ No   Negative beliefs about oneself, others and
                the world and about the cause or conse-
                quences of the event
❒ Yes ❒ No   Feeling detached from other people
❒ Yes ❒ No   Inability to feel positive emotions
❒ Yes ❒ No   Persistent negative emotional state

Are you troubled by at least two of the following?

❒ Yes ❒ No   Problems sleeping
❒ Yes ❒ No   Irritability or outbursts of anger
❒ Yes ❒ No   Reckless or self-destructive behavior
❒ Yes ❒ No   Problems concentrating
❒ Yes ❒ No   Feeling "on guard"
❒ Yes ❒ No   An exaggerated startle response

> ### Ray of Light
>
> Visualize. Picture divine white light coming through the crown of your head and darkness flowing out the bottom of your feet. This reduces stress by moving anxious energy out of your body.

Living with Someone with PTSD

Dr. Janet Seahorn, Tony's wife, shared what it's like living with someone with PTSD.[29] They co-wrote a book, *Tears of a Warrior: A Family's Story of Combat and Living with PTSD.* They've received thousands of letters, emails, and phone calls primarily from veterans and people such as first responders who've suffered from PTSD. As Tony shares his personal story, Janet shares her perspective as a mother and spouse. In turn, readers get to see firsthand not only the physical but the mental scars of combat.

Dr. Seahorn believes that PTSD is an equal opportunity destroyer affecting combat vets, people who have undergone a lot of personal trauma, cancer victims, and sometimes even pregnant women when they go through childbirth.

Janet Seahorn, PhD

So many people struggling from trauma feel that they can't get over it because they lack courage, strength, coping mechanisms. It turns out it is none of those things. It is something that has happened in the brain. The brain has reorganized itself so people could survive these very horrible things. And that is a gift. Now you have to figure out ways to deal with this different new brain that you have in order to be more functional. And that, I think, has been the biggest gift of writing our book, is that people were just going around feeling guilty and feeling unable to cope because they weren't strong enough to be able to overcome these traumas. And that was absolutely not true.[30]

As a trauma survivor or a spouse or family member of someone with PTSD, we may not realize to what extent trauma affects our daily lives. To help determine the impact, the Seahorns created two sets of PTSD questions in their book. One is for the veteran and the other one is for family and loved ones of the veteran. Note that although this was designed for veterans, the questions apply to anyone suffering from PTSD. Your responses may reveal how much your life has changed since you were traumatized.

Questions Veteran*		
Veterans	Give Examples	Coping Strategies
Am I as close to others as I was before serving in combat? Y N		
When working or talking, how do I respond to those closest to me? Y N		
Do I listen to my spouse and children without always interrupting? Y N		
Do I speak clearly—stating my needs without blame or anger? Y N		
What experiences do I share with my spouse or significant other? Why? Y N		

Veterans	Give Examples	Coping Strategies
What experiences do I not share? Why?		
Do I have trouble falling or staying asleep? Y N		
Am I more on edge and irritable? Y N		
Am I feeling socially isolated and alone? Y N		
Am I easily distracted and have a difficult time concentrating? Y N		
Am I less joyful and able to enjoy life as I was before combat? Y N		
How many times did you answer Yes? _____ No? _____		

* (or others dealing with PTSD) ©Tears of a Warrior (reprinted with

permission)

Questions Spouse/Family Member		
Spouse/Family Member	Give Examples	Coping Strategies
Am I as close to my vet as I was before his/her combat duty? Y N		
How does my vet respond to my needs, concerns?		
Do I listen to my vet with an open mind to understand what he/she is/has experienced? Y N		
Do I speak clearly— stating my needs without blame or anger? Y N		
Do I thoughtfully listen when my vet is sharing personal feelings and information with me? Y N		

Spouse/Family Member	Give Examples	Coping Strategies
Do I have trouble falling and/or staying asleep? Y N		
Am I more on edge and irritable? Y N		
Am I feeling socially isolated and alone? Y N		
Am I more easily distracted and have a difficult time concentrating? Y N		
Am I less joyful and able to enjoy life since my vet's return from combat? Y N		
How many times did you answer Yes? _____ No? _____		

©Tears of a Warrior (reprinted with permission)

Whether you are a spouse, family member, or have PTSD, are you surprised at your responses? Many people are. Their behaviors have become the "new normal." They just never realize the changes as they were happening. There's no denying it; long after trauma happens, we are still haunted by it. Dr. Seahorn has witnessed this over and over.

Fishing in the Wisdom Well

In 1980, the American Psychiatric Association (APA) added PTSD to the third edition of its Diagnostic and Statistical Manual of Mental Disorders (DSM-III) manual.[31]

Speak Up and Set Strong Boundaries

Setting boundaries is about communicating with others on how you'd like to be treated taking into consideration what you value most. There are both healthy and unhealthy boundaries. An example of a healthy boundary is noticing and speaking up when someone invades your boundary. Unhealthy boundaries include expecting others to anticipate and fulfill your needs.

Janet Seahorn, PhD

Before PTSD became an official diagnosis, the way we dealt with it was we didn't deal with it. We just kept making the same mistakes over and over again. As a spouse living with someone with PTSD, I formed boundaries such as no physical, emotional or verbal abuse from day one. I don't care whether that person is suffering from post-traumatic stress, or something else. In any healthy relationship, you have to have solid boundaries that state, "These are the things that I will not tolerate. If you cross that line, maybe I'll forgive you once, but you'll never get a second chance unless the person shows that he/she is working to change it." And that has to be followed very strictly.

If you dismiss and keep accepting that behavior, what you are actually saying is this person isn't good enough, strong enough, and isn't worthy enough of getting better. And that absolutely is wrong. When you love somebody, you want the best for them. We will address it as it comes up, but we will not dismiss it. We will not stick our heads in the sand and say, "Everything is just fine when it isn't fine." Every time something inappropriate happens, it is basically making that crack in a relationship bigger and bigger, which is why so many relationships fail. I wish we had information on Post Traumatic Stress in the beginning of our marriage. There certainly are things we would have done differently had we been aware of what we were dealing with at the time.[32]

Healing Takes Work

There is a common saying that time heals all wounds. With PTSD, that idiom does not apply. Sometimes you have to work on managing those wounds.

People want healing, especially emotional healing, to be painless. That's just not the way our minds and bodies work. Healing is painful. It takes work and there are days when you make progress and days that you take some steps backward. It's getting up each day and addressing specific issues and moving forward.

It's important for people to know how dangerous PTSD is. If you deal with it, you can manage it. You might even be lucky enough to cure it. But, if you don't deal with it, it's probably not going to go away on its own. If it doesn't, the damage you're going to do to others will be significant. Maybe if you don't deal with it, you'll survive, but people that come in contact with you may not. It's each person's responsibility to do what they can to get better.

PTSD and Complex PTSD

PTSD is sometimes described as being "complex." What's the difference? Typically, PTSD is related to one event. In contrast, complex PTSD (CPTSD) is related to a series of events, or one prolonged event. Symptoms of PTSD can happen after a traumatic episode, such as a car accident, sexual assault, or something related to mother nature like a tornado, hurricane, or wildfire. CPTSD is often seen in refugees, people held in captivity such as prostitutes, people dealing with long-term domestic violence, among many others. As an adult, the longer the traumatic exposure the greater the chance of having CPTSD which is considered a type of anxiety disorder. Common symptoms of PTSD *and* CPTSD include the following:

Reliving the trauma through flashbacks and nightmares

Avoiding situations that remind them of the trauma

Feeling dizzy or nauseated when remembering the trauma

Experiencing hyperarousal, or being in a continual state of high alert

Believing the world is a dangerous place

Losing trust in self or others

Difficulty sleeping or concentrating

Being startled by loud noises

People with PTSD *or* CPTSD may also experience:

A negative self-view. CPTSD can cause a person to view themselves negatively and feel helpless, guilty, or ashamed. They often consider themselves to be different from other people.

Changes in beliefs and worldview. People with either condition may hold a negative view of the world and the people in it or lose faith in previously held beliefs.

Emotional regulation difficulties. These conditions can cause people to lose control over their emotions. They may experience intense anger or sadness or have thoughts of suicide.

Relationship issues. Relationships may suffer due to difficulties trusting and interacting, and because of a negative self-view. A person with either condition may develop unhealthy relationships because they are what the person has known in the past.

Detachment from the trauma. A person may dissociate, or feel detached from emotions or physical sensations. Some people completely forget the trauma.

Preoccupation with an abuser. It is not uncommon to fixate on the abuser, the relationship with the abuser, or getting revenge for the abuse.

Symptoms of complex PTSD can vary, and they may change over time. People with the condition may also experience symptoms that are not listed above.[33]

Human Trafficking and Complex PTSD

Jennifer Jamison, APSW, is a therapist and social worker in Appleton, Wisconsin, who was featured in our film *Light in the Darkness*. She advocates against human trafficking. Jamison shared the following:

"Working with trafficking victims is intense because of their multifaceted needs, which are often compounded by the effects of Complex PTSD (CPTSD). Caused by multiple incidences of trauma—often interpersonal in nature—CPTSD is like PTSD on steroids. Also, while PTSD is fear based, CPTSD is often based in shame.

Trafficking victims experience shame from multiple sources, including their trafficker and a society that condemns their behavior. Only survivors can understand what that feels like."

In *Light in the Darkness*, Jenny Jamison described how CPTSD plays out in the world of human trafficking:

Jennifer Jamison, APSW

CPTSD involves severe, persistent or cumulative abuse. There's also a high correlation with what is called high betrayal trauma. High betrayal trauma happens when somebody a person knows or trusts is the perpetrator – compounding the damage. Victims may feel they are being trapped, or perceive they are not going to be able to escape this and being rescued is not likely. This can lead to trauma bonding as well as suicide attempts because they feel they really have no way out.

Like PTSD, a person doesn't have to experience the abuse to develop CPTSD. In addition to those who have experienced human trafficking, populations who report high rates of CPTSD include prisoners of war, refugees, asylum seekers, and those who grew up in civil unrest, war trauma, or genocide. My mom's parents grew up in Holland during World War II and lived underground for a portion of their childhood. At a young age, my grandpa was dragging dead bodies off the field. I never knew him as he died before I was born, but I believe this was the reason he became an alcoholic.

Another element of CPTSD is that it can be often unplanned. Like a prisoner of war, their torture is unplanned. Traffickers are notoriously so manipulative. They isolate their victims and use manipulation tactics. Books have been written on how to "break" the women in your stable and keep them under control. In cities like Milwaukee, Wisconsin they have round tables where they all get together and discuss tactics. They might even switch up women who are causing trouble. One woman I met had a trafficker use what was referred to as the "hot and cold treatment" on her. She had to get naked and go into a bathtub full of ice cubes. He then lit a cigarette and let it burn – without smoking it. She couldn't get out until the cigarette was all ash. She felt like she was going to die in that bathtub.

There are some traffickers who use drugs to keep their girls as what they refer to as a "leash." This way, they don't need to struggle to control them, rather, the drugs keep them from doing this.

Stockholm Syndrome is when people like hostages develop a psychological alliance with their captors during captivity. The term is most associated with Patty Hearst, the Californian newspaper heiress who was kidnapped by revolutionary militants in 1974. She appeared to develop sympathy with her captors and joined them in a robbery. She was eventually caught and received a prison sentence. But Hearst's defense lawyer claimed that the 19-year-old had been brainwashed and was suffering from "Stockholm Syndrome." I see it as our brains switching on a survival mechanism. It's your brain saying if I don't switch, I'm gonna die. I've met several women who were trafficked and arrested — causing them to be isolated from their trafficker. And they said that was one of the best things that could've happened because it gave them time to think and assess what this person was doing to them. It helped loosen those trauma bonds.

There's this insidious nature of trauma where it's accompanied by shame, or worthlessness, feelings of failure, diminished sense of self, which is interestingly enough similar to one of the criteria for Borderline Personality Disorder. This also comes with difficulty in maintaining or sustaining interpersonal relationships or feeling legitimately close to other people.

With human trafficking, you might think that the sex buyers are pedophiles because they seek out young girls. But these men are usually situational abusers propelled by the high and a society that sexualizes girls. For trafficking victims that have been trafficked at a young age of 12 or 13, if they get out of trafficking at age 20, they don't have an education, fundamental life skills, and they essentially have to learn everything they missed out on. There is some literature on working with this population but it's complicated – every person's needs are different. Something we've known for a while is that our bodies hold trauma.[34]

Ray of Light

Practice self-compassion. Your thoughts make a difference. Be sweet to yourself whenever possible—avoid beating yourself up. Remember to show yourself compassion when you're stressed or emotionally distraught. Replacing negative thoughts with positive ones enhances your well-being. Incorporate actionable steps that reinforce your affirmations.

The Human Tiger Factor

Peter Levine, Ph.D., developed Somatic Experiencing, a method of listening to the body to heal from trauma and other stress disorders. His book *Waking the Tiger: Healing Trauma* is published in twenty-two languages. This visionary book offers a new and hopeful vision to recovering from trauma. Just like tigers, Levine views humans as unique and instinctual.

The author asks the question, "Why are animals in the wild, though they are threatened often, rarely traumatized?" By taking the time to understand how animals are immune to these traumatic symptoms, he's able to solve the mystery. What does he discover? By paying attention and focusing on body sensations, it's possible to heal.

Jack Kornfield, Ph.D., author, activist, and trained Buddhist monk, wrote a report entitled "How Mindfulness Can Break the Cycle of Fear and Anger." In it, Dr. Kornfield stated:

Fear is a natural thing. It is an organism's way of trying to protect itself, but as human beings, we can spin-out a great deal with it. I teach people how to sit and acknowledge the fear as if to bow to it—pay respect—because it's very powerful. How does it feel in the body? What are the stories that it tells? Are they true or not? What are the emotions that come with it? . . . The image from Buddhist psychology is if you put a teaspoon of salt in a cup of water, it tastes very salty, but if you put the same spoon of salt in a lake, the water is pure and clear. In the same way, you can make the heart more spacious and open and gracious so that fear and confusion are held in a spacious heart . . . To be present and to learn, to train oneself in mindfulness, or to offer it to others, you can only offer that if you've really found this capacity in yourself.[35]

DeEtte Ranae: From PTSD Survivor to Healer

DeEtte Ranae is a PTSD survivor and a healer. She is also a certified psychic medium and master teacher of Psychic Mediumship Development. DeEtte's childhood was fraught with violence and abuse. Her mother was pregnant with her in high school and her parents had a "shotgun wedding," which her father never wanted.

DeEtte remembers being thrown in the crib by her father before her first birthday. She recalls in very graphic detail being molested by a family member around age four or five. At age thirteen, she attempted suicide. As she entered into adulthood, she found herself in abusive relationships.

Over the years, she had hundreds of hours of therapy. Nothing worked, including taking prescribed medications. When she became interested in psychic mediumship and wanted to get her master certification, she was told she needed to heal herself first before helping others. Journaling helped but brought up a lot of uncomfortable memories. It wasn't until she studied Spirits that she was able to heal.

On the Road to Becoming a Healer

DeEtte knew from a young age that she was gifted; she always seemed to know things that others did not. As she got older, she found a passion in helping others as she wanted to aid in their healing. She went to nursing school and then became a Reiki master-teacher. She spent part of her adolescence and adult life learning all she could about Spirits and communication with loved ones who had passed.

Through her studies she found her path to help others heal mentally, emotionally, physically, and spiritually. She uses her gifts as a medical intuitive to connect with clients and bring Spirit forth, as healing comes in messages from loved ones, guides, and the loving energy of the universe. (Note that mediumship is the practice of mediating communication between spirits of the dead and living human beings. Practitioners are known as "mediums" or "spirit mediums.")

Fishing from the Wisdom Well

Most American adults self-identify as Christians. But many Christians also hold what are sometimes characterized as "New Age" beliefs – including belief in reincarnation, astrology, psychics and the presence of spiritual energy in physical objects such as mountains or trees. About six out of ten American adults accept at least one New Age belief. Four out of ten people believe in psychics and that spiritual energy can be found in physical objects, while somewhat smaller numbers express belief in reincarnation (33%) and astrology (29%).[36]

DeEtte Ranae Shares the Importance of Spirit in Her Life

Most people don't want to deal with painful memories; they try to suppress them. I literally re-lived all my memories through Spirit but then made sense of them. By doing so, I realized there's a reason why I'm a medium. My whole life is like a library for Spirit to use. As I began doing readings for people, Spirit would show me that I'm talking to somebody who's been molested, attempted suicide, or has been in these abusive relationships. And then in return, I'm able to help them as I went through the same thing."

At age nine, I started having dreams of people's deaths. So, within a week of having a dream that somebody had died, they would die. The first one was my grandma. She came to me in a dream when she was in the hospital. She was talking about death. At that age, I had never been in a hospital because you needed to be at least age thirteen. My grandma's soul took me to all these rooms and then opened up this door and it was her body. She had all these tubes and hoses coming out of her nose and an IV. I recognized her as my grandma at that point. That's when she explained to me the difference between body and soul.

She told me her body wasn't working anymore and she was going to leave it behind and to not be afraid. I told her that I wasn't going to be afraid anymore. After her body was gone, I could talk to her the rest of my life. Then she told me that I had the ability to talk to spirits and that my life journey would involve doing this. When I woke up in the morning, I told my mom that grandma had died. My mom told me to shut up as she did not die. And 10 minutes later she got the phone call.

If it wasn't for Spirit and this life path, I would still be the mess that I was. I can guarantee you that. When you have trauma, you don't realize how sick you are. I was a serious mess. I didn't take vacations. I worked 24/7 and barely knew who my kids were. I didn't take time for me. So, if Spirit didn't come in and put me back on this path that I was supposed to live, my life would not have purpose now. [37]

The Serenity Prayer
God, grant me the serenity to accept the
things I cannot change,
courage to change the things I can,
and wisdom to know the difference.

–Reinhold Niebuhr

The intention of the Serenity Prayer is to bring peace, faith, and certainty to the hearts and minds of those seeking God's support. It asks God for the wisdom and the ability to gracefully accept "what is" (what cannot be changed) and for the willingness to manifest, with

God's support, that which is in one's highest good. The following is an adaptation for someone exposed to trauma and PTSD:

Grant me the serenity to accept the things I cannot change: the past, what happened to me, that what happened was traumatic no matter how effectively I have stuffed it.

Courage to change the things I can: my attitude towards my symptoms—help me to accept them as a normal response to trauma and evidence that I need to take care of myself by talking about this and getting help; my actions—I no longer have to drug or deny my symptoms. I can just accept them: my reactions— instead of freaking out I can focus on the symptom, feel what I feel, go through, and deal with, the pain and learn whatever it is that my Higher Power wants me to know and share about the effects of trauma on people. Finally I can change how I see these symptoms—as normal and helpful to me in my recovery even if they are painful. Eventually I will be able to help other people who share a history of trauma.

And the wisdom to know the difference: I can change my actions and reactions. Help me to be willing, teachable, and to learn about myself and what I have survived even if it is frightening.

Prayer for People with Trauma and PTSD

Higher Power, I know that it's not within the harmony of the universe that I be healed from the trauma of remembering _____(traumatic incidents) without pain. Help me through the pain. Surround me with the golden light of healing, fill me with the white light of peace and love. Help me to bear the pain as I go through these memories. Help me to cry. Help me to remember. Help me to love myself no matter what happened to me or what I did to survive. Help me to release and to let go of my survival skills, the things such as anger and numbness that helped keep me alive, as I become aware of how ineffective they can be in getting me what I want today. Fill me with light and love until I am green and growing again in the harmony of the universe, if it be thy will. Amen.[38]

This modified version is a testament to us that life is a series of choices and what we have found by creating this compendium of awareness within our films and books is that in order to reach most of humanity with our message, that message has to resonate on a Spiritual level of Universal truth. We believe humans are innately good. By encouraging others (and ourselves) to have the fortitude to heal the wounds we have acquired along the path is why we created our film *Light in the Darkness* and this book. Lifting the stigma has never been a bigger conversation than it is right now. Human beings have the capacity to be resilient and strong at the same time they are vulnerable and delicate. The human condition is a miracle.

Note all the resources listed here can be accessed on https://consciouscontent.org by clicking on the Wisdom Well Resources link.

THE WISDOM WELL

Reading:

Janet and Anthony Seahorn. *Tears of a Warrior: A Family's Story of Combat and Living with PTSD*. Fort Collins, CO: Team Pursuits Publishing, 2008. This patriotic book was written about soldiers who are called to duty to serve their country. It shows how PTSD affects the veteran, family and how to restore hope by implementing strategies for living with PTSD.

Heyman, M., Dill, J. Douglas, R. 2018. *Ruderman White Paper on Mental Health and Suicide of First Responders*. Reveals that more first responders commit suicide than die in the line of duty. Makes a case for why first responders need to take care of their mental health.

Levine, Peter. *Waking the Tiger: Healing Trauma.* Berkeley, CA: North Atlantic Books, 1997. This historic book compares the human and wild animal's response to trauma and discovers how we humans can learn from animals when getting past our own trauma.

"For trafficking victims, leaving is never easy." An article from Oshkosh Northwestern dated Sept. 18, 2016. Since the average age of entry into sex trafficking is 13, victims are deprived basic life experiences, and girls who want to get out of prostitution typically don't have the necessary job skills, education or family support.

Court Records Detail Group's Sex Trafficking "Pimp Roundables". This article from the Milwaukee-Wisconsin Journal Sentinel shares how a Milwaukee man, described by prosecutors as a pimp who taught his teenage son how to sexually exploit women, regularly participated in "pimp roundtables".

"What is Stockholm Syndrome?" This BBC News article looks at the origins of how the term The Stockholm Syndrome was coined.

"Trauma Bonding and Trafficking." This journal article looks at how to deal with a trauma bond once someone is no longer a sex trafficker.

Watching/Listening:

"Some Gave Love," (4:03) a video by Billy Cyrus honoring our veterans explaining how some veterans gave some while others gave all.

"Prostitution - A Difficult Job to Escape" (13:00) For many prostitutes, the prospect of escaping the industry seems impossible or at the very least too dangerous to endure. Jackie McReynolds is a former prostitute and now executive director of the Angels Project Power, a program that helps women leave prostitution. McReynolds explains how the program works and Nakita Harrison, who is enrolled in the project, shares her experience and her attempt to turn her life around.

"Human Trafficking Victims and the Brain" (20:49) Andy Soper talks about how brains of sex traffickers are changed because of the trauma associated with it.

"Inside the Mindset of Sex Trafficking Victims" (6:34) Dr. Chitra Raghavan describes signs and symptoms of sex trafficking victims and the main, problematic emotion of 'feeling responsible for the abusers future' in her study 'Trauma-coerced Bonding and Victims of Sex Trafficking:

Where do we go from here?'

"Pimpology: The 48 Laws of the Game" (audio book) is a book authored by Pimpin' Ken. The pimp has reached nearly mythical status. This guy from the ghetto with no startup capital and no credit - nothing but the words out of his mouth - comes not only to have a stable of sexy women who consider him "their man", but to drive a Rolls, sport diamonds, and wear custom suits and alligator shoes from Italy. His secret is to follow the "unwritten rules of the game."

"Stopping Traffic Film." The film is a call to action, intending to inspire the viewer to join in the movement to seek an end to human trafficking, helping to break the isolation of millions of voiceless victims.

Taking Action:

Take a free assessment from *Psychology Today* on personality, IQ, relationships, personality, or health. Popular assessments include mental health, depression, anxiety, career assessment and more.

Take a free mental health assessment from PsychCentral. Includes an Anxiety Screening Test, a Coronavirus Anxiety Scale, ADD test, and more to assess your mental health.

Visit www.tearsofawarrior.com, Janet and Anthony Seahorn's webpage that shares many valuable resources for veterans including an opportunity to purchase their book, *Tears of a Warrior*.

Join *My PTSD Forum*, which was launched with one simple aim, to provide quality PTSD information and support to all concerned. The community is about getting down to the nitty gritty, talking about the issues, learning from each other, and at the end of the day, hopefully lead a more rewarding and stress-free life.

Order free US government brochures/posters/magnets about PTSD, You can print the brochures on your own computer or order copies of material that deal with all aspects of PTSD for both PTSD survivors and loved ones.

Visit the National Institute for the Clinical Application of Behavioral Medicine. Although this website is for clinicians, has some great material and infographics that help explain trauma and why it's so hard to recover from it.

Visit Blue Knot Foundation, the National Centre of Excellence for Complex trauma. Even though this website is based in Australia, they have great resources for survivors, family, friends and loved ones. Some great videos too that are less than 11 minutes.

Connect with Psychic, Medium, and Medical Intuitive DeEtte Ranae via her webpage. She does in person readings as well as through Skype, Zoom, and via the phone.

PART II

Grief:
Unfoldment of the Plan

The only way out of grief is through the feelings.

-Brian Ross

This chapter wasn't in our original plan, but after we learned about the correlation between grief and PTSD and went through some unexpected grief of our own, we felt it was crucial to include it in this book. As each day passes, we seem to collect bits of wisdom as we begin to create space between ourselves and the event. We want to share that process with you. It's part of the unfoldment of the plan.

When Grief Happens - Kimberly Resch

My family is doing the best they can to work through this very real set of circumstances we have been given without a manual.

Add a quarantine on top of that, misinformation, and fear. All of that can make for a really sticky sad environment to be spending time in my house. I was just feet from where my son's lifeless body had lain, and I was stuck seeing that pool in front of me every day. We weren't allowed to go anywhere unless it was an emergency and ironically the one day we were gone for only 55 minutes, the accident happened.

I had to make peace with it, bless this last place he was, and not let it set in or it would have been a mental disaster of no return in my mind. Already having PTSD, this was adding another layer to my healing regimen. This time it felt way bigger than what I was capable of managing. The grief management and release is a daily conversation I have within myself.

I have been a healing practitioner for the last twelve years. Of all of the resources that I have, I couldn't find one that I could use when I was in trauma shock resulting from the loss of my son, Taylor.

Grieving requires grace and time. When you grieve, you might tell yourself you should be fine. You think things like, *As the mom, I have to be strong for everyone else because I hold the family together.* When you decide you "should be" a certain way, you're buying into the prevailing stigma surrounding grief. And you can miss out on the healing.

I am almost positive grieving is necessary for the long-term healing process. Our friend Annah Pelot presented the term "unfoldment" to us. Unfoldment is a noun meaning the gradual development or revelation of something. Let the unfoldment begin.

The positive influences and reintegration of energies from our past have created support we may have forgotten was available to us. As a woman, relationships with other women have been difficult for me until I met my long-lost sisters of light, Dr. Kari Uselman and Annah Pelot during my Shamanic journey. They have held space for not only myself but also are an intricate part of Brian's healing process.

They have helped us to establish the foundation and support from the Spiritual world we had failed to call upon in the trauma state we were living in. I hadn't connected to them in nearly seven years as our paths took us down different roads of healing and experience. The day I made my first post on social media about Taylor's passing, Annah responded and further stated she felt "called" by Taylor to rise up and help guide this process in whatever way was necessary.

While writing and editing this book, both Kari and Annah have been an integral part of organizing it. The information they have access to is not readily available to the public. It's an ancient wisdom that is carried in both of these women as messengers. Brian and I often receive messages from them reminding us of God's support and to be open to the gifts he can provide us. Their calling to assist us on our journey to complete this book and navigate the healing process with us was a divine intervention. Over a seven-day period we accomplished an insurmountable mission to change the direction of this book and live in 100 percent truth and authenticity. At this point, I was beginning to see the unfoldment of the divine plan.

Making Sense of Grief

Grief is messy. It doesn't go in some linear order where you start out sad and miraculously come out happy a few months later. Can we say it again? Grief is real messy.

Elisabeth Kübler-Ross' groundbreaking book *On Death and Dying* describes five stages of grief: (1) denial; (2) anger; (3) bargaining; (4) depression; and 5) acceptance. She'd be the first to admit that grief is complicated and doesn't progress from stage one to five in a specific time period. In fact, you can go through all five stages of grief rather rapidly or get stuck in one stage for a long time. But Kübler-Ross was right. There are different stages of grief, and she put a label on each stage.

David Kessler is a grief and loss specialist who has co-authored books with Kübler-Ross. He created Grief.com to help others deal with grief. In a podcast with author Brené Brown, Ph.D., he shared, "Judgment of each other's grieving causes a divorce. The loss of a child doesn't cause a divorce. We don't grieve exactly alike. Two people with an empty tank can't fill each other up. There's not a bypass through the pain. You will be in pain. If you don't feel it, you can't heal it."[39]

> Our grief is as unique as our fingerprint.
> We all have different backgrounds of love,
> and we all approach grief in our own ways.[40]
>
> –David Kessler, grief specialist, author

Feeling Unprepared - Kimberly's POV

Back in January 2020, I didn't know I would be a recipient of grieving in real time. I had a compelling story alone from my childhood that was slated for this part. It has taken a lot of personal development and work to get to this point. In March 2020, as my world is crumbling, I am asked to dig deep and share my processing of Taylor's death publicly. Writing this book and knowing this chapter was an important part of the plan, I am realizing this may go down as one of the most challenging tasks I have ever done. Mentally, I have had to work at creating a safe space in my head to go into those dark places no one wants to go.

My education in Emotional Intelligence and history of Shamanism still didn't prepare me for that day and all of these days after. Cherie Lindberg, LPC, a Brianspotting educator and counselor featured in our film *Light in the Darkness*, asked me to write it all down and talk about it when I felt I could. Brian and I met with her the day after Taylor's accident. Everything and everyone was just spinning out of control as I tried to figure out how to cope with this loss. We immediately put the kids into counseling so they would have an outlet. I have been documenting everything since that fateful day in March, and you will read a few of my entries below.

Having PTSD from being held at gunpoint and witnessing a murder-suicide when I was ten was a life-altering experience I have carried with me. This event created its own set of challenges growing up and dealing with life. It was only a few years ago that I started the healing process from that event. However, the loss of a child—that's a different category altogether.

As a mom, I had to come to acknowledge the unthinkable, which was never seeing my child Taylor, who had been in my life for 5,720 days, again. As important as that fact was, I really needed to figure out how to continue living in a state of awareness and gratitude for the remaining time of my life and wondered if this tragedy would resurface any of my previous trauma and how I would deal with that.

> Don't judge your loved one's grief response. Give them the freedom to grieve their own way and hold yourself and them in grace and patience during the healing process.
>
> —Kimberly Resch, author, filmmaker

I have dug so deep within myself and have been inspired and challenged by adversity since I can remember, always rising up and going the extra mile to give my all. Trying to accomplish the near impossible. In fact, accomplishing the impossible was a motto of mine. In this experience with Taylor, my youngest, I saw two choices regarding my new reality: Either I bury myself in the distraught sadness I had never experienced before without a roadmap back or use the legacy of my amazing child who had just crossed over to fuel me to continue to tell the story and help others along the way as he did while he was alive.

I had to choose a direction. Every day, I was in limbo emotionally. His passing was a death sentence for my soul. Understanding all too well how PTSD can work into your day-to-day existence, creating stories and leaving you not quite right, was a reality I was already experiencing. I have been determined to be mindful and allow myself to really feel my catastrophe so that PTSD would not be my future and that unfinished processing wouldn't be connected to my son's passing.

Meeting with a brainspotting professional (a therapist who believes the direction in which you look or gaze can affect the way you feel) and alternative medicine practitioners—who were not only compassionate, but excellent at their craft—to help me along when I got stuck was a lifesaver for sure. Filing my memories in the correct place and talking and writing about the experience even though it was painful was imperative to prevent additional brain tissue damage. So I opted to just lean in and let it pass through me so that I could heal without fear or a lingering negative effect. Taylor was literally my "light" reflection. He had so many plans. As a teenager, he was already doing the work required to leave a legacy.

Taylor was fifteen when he passed, and it was impressive to witness the impression he had made on the thousands of people who reached out after his death. Well after his passing, he was still receiving thousands of messages on social media. It's heartbreaking to know his young friends were reaching out saying things like "I miss you so much, just come back" or "I do the hard work for you Taylor, keep grinding in heaven, miss you bro" and even dedicating their senior speech to the loss of a friend missed so much by so many in the community.

He was close with his dad, Andrew; his grandmother's Ann and Dawn, Brian, his mentor, his brothers Zach and Cody, 6 and 13 years older, Morgan and Ashlee, his sisters by another mother, and his girlfriend, Lexi. I feel I should mention all of his soccer family as well. Their outpouring of support was really important for his dad, Andrew. They both lived on the soccer field. Taylor's dad and grandma were at every game and put thousands of miles on their vehicles to take him where he needed to go without complaining. All of these people defined his life with love and challenges to allow him to exercise his ability to be compassionate, sweet, and competitive. As a parent, I couldn't have wished for more.

It still baffles me that I am even writing these words. Brian and I often talk about there being a crack in the matrix that day. Nothing has been the same since. In fact, during this time, the pandemic turned everyone else's life upside down too.

I feel sometimes I have entered into a different dimension and that my life I knew is somewhere waiting for my return because this year of 2020 has been over the top ridiculous and devastating for the countless masses. I have learned so much from my tragic experiences and have immense gratitude for the human condition.

Kimberly and the Stages of Grief

I thought that I would go through each of the five stages of grief one at a time and know which stage I was in and how much further I had to go. If you ask those who have gone through devastating losses, that simply isn't true. Honestly, you can go through all of those stages within an hour and be okay for a couple hours until something else happens and the process starts over again like a terrible version of the movie *Groundhog Day*.

This process is exhausting when it happens eighteen or twenty-four hours a day several in a row. You feel like roadkill. Your lungs start to give out from the continuous hyperventilating, your voice cracks, your eyes tear so much that you can't actually read what you're trying to write, and they ache from crying.

Being human is so special because we can "love" so hard to trigger this reaction. For me, the most magical part of being human is our ability to love both ourselves and others this much. For the limited time we get to live in our bodies, is the best attribute we have.

It's surprising how physical grief can be. Your heart literally aches. A memory comes up that causes your stomach to clench or a chill to run down your spine. Some nights, your mind races, and your heart races along with it, your body so electrified with energy that you can barely sleep. Other nights, you're so tired that you fall asleep right away. You wake up the next morning still feeling exhausted and spend most of the day in bed.

–Stephanie Hairston, WebMD Special Report

In this chapter, Brian and I share our grief in real time. It is important to note that we are moving through our grief differently. In this section, we share snippets of that grief with the hope it will help others heal too. Although our grieving isn't over, we're ready to share our story with you.

The date and time our world changed: Thursday, March 26, 2020, at 3:50 p.m. EST. It was a sunny day in Oviedo, Florida.

Tragedy Meets Truth

On March 26, 2020, our fifteen-year-old son drowned from a phenomenon called "shallow water blackout" in our pool. Shallow Water Blackout, brought on by holding your breath for long periods of time, is an underwater "faint" due to the lack of oxygen to the brain. He had been performing a Wim Hof Method Breathing Technique (designed to boost energy and increase endurance) while sitting on the ledge of the deep side of the pool and then timing himself underwater.

Taylor was an unlikely candidate for drowning. He was an excellent swimmer and athlete and had previously been on the swim team. He was always pushing himself to be better, go longer, and be stronger. But the prolonged lack of oxygen caused his brain to shut down without warning, and he went into immediate cardiac arrest.

Two weeks into the pandemic, Brian and I had gone to the store for approximately fifty-five minutes. Before leaving, we told the kids that we would be gone a short while. Between our kids and their friends, we had several teenagers in the house and all of them were out by the pool pretty much all day, every day.

We were aware that Taylor had been doing the Wim Hof Method, even though he hadn't done these breathing techniques in front of us. Common sense says you should never do that type of deep breathing technique near water, and we had never witnessed him crossing that line. We think he tried to stay under the water for three to five minutes to break his own record; the YouTube video suggests you can hold your breath for up to five minutes if you do it correctly. From what his friends later told us, Taylor used this process to increase his lung capacity on dry land, and someone was always with him to time him.

This time was different, and Taylor fell unconscious. It was an error in judgment made by his juvenile brain. He wasn't being careful or asking for help or to even be timed while performing this technique. Whether he fell from the pool ledge step and dropped in headfirst or was already under the water timing himself when this happened, we don't know. But once he was unconscious, water filled his lungs and he sank to the bottom facing upward.

We arrived home five minutes after his best friend, who was visiting him from Wisconsin, came looking for him to play basketball and found him at the bottom of the pool. Thinking his unresponsiveness was a cruel joke, he jumped into the water and tried to move him. Once he realized what was happening, he came up for air, dove back down to retrieve Taylor, and placed him on his back on the lanai.

He ran out to where we were in the garage with bags in our hands; we dropped everything and rushed to the pool. Brian and I performed CPR for more than ten minutes while his friend called 911. We took turns doing chest compressions and mouth-to-mouth resuscitation. But Taylor was blue and unresponsive and his lungs completely saturated with water. The EMT's arrived and after assessing him determined there was nothing they could do—no paddles, no CPR. Taylor had no pulse and the best guess was that he had been without oxygen for too long. He was gone.

I was pulling myself together and calling his dad, 1,300 miles away, to tell him the most important person in his life had died on my watch. I was shattered from the inside out. He provided me grace and patience when we spoke and that really helped me to not spiral further into despair.

> We do not have control over many things in life and death but we do have control over the meaning we give it.
>
> –Nathalie Himmelrich, author *Grieving Parents: Surviving Loss as a Couple* [41]

The following are some of my private journal entries and Facebook posts starting the morning after Taylor's death. I'm sharing them here because I'm hopeful they can be helpful to anyone dealing with grief.

> The Body is temporary, your Soul though, it propelled through all of us with a lasting impression of love here on earth. May you Rest In Peace my beautiful boy! Forever in my heart and everyday was a blessing to have been in your presence. You are the most beautiful gift and the 494,208,000 seconds 8,236,800 minutes 137,280 hours 5720 days 817 weeks and 1 day I have been given to be your

mom I will cherish forever. Thank you for picking me! You are deeply loved and missed Taylor.

March 27, 2020

On day two after Taylor's death, Brian and I had a brainspotting counseling session with Cherie Lindberg, it was more like a session where Cherie held space for us to incoherently use words that didn't make any sense in between crying. She said this was normal given the circumstances. We video recorded it for reviewing it later if we felt compelled and even though we were in trauma shock, she explained that we were where we needed to be in the healing process. She explained this was the beginning of an integration process. I know our minds were still simulating the information and trying to figure out where to put it early on. I think we both felt mostly sad and cried, sometimes at different times, sometimes together.

I am recalling the images of what happened playing over and over even with my eyes open. Then I had moments of numbness and disbelief. The three hours of relief later that night probably were helpful as I was in denial. I couldn't eat anything. My very healthy appetite was literally non-existent. I tried reliving all the signs I never saw that morning or maybe the past and negotiated what I could have done differently a hundred different ways to prevent what happened to Taylor. As a parent, I felt like a failure. My practical self knows this was an accident and there was nothing I could have done differently that day as there weren't any signs of distress. I was literally having a conversation with him an hour before and his light was bright as usual.

Our rational self knows that if we could have saved him, we would have. But when you are in trauma shock, you tend to negotiate your way through it to somehow make yourself feel worse. Those images are relentless. This isn't productive, I promise you, however, apparently it's part of grief. Your loved one can't speak to you, it's just silence. What's done is done and a feeling of helplessness takes over.

For an overachiever, I find this silence unacceptable. In that silence, your mind can run away with half truths, inaccurate perspectives and guilt. This just perpetuates more chaos. When I started to write the Facebook post about Taylor's passing it allowed me some space. With every word I wrote, I breathed a little bit better.

April 1, 2020

Life lessons are a tricky thing. They mold us and shift us inside to reflect what we have truly learned in this earth school. Taylor Jennings graduated and is on his next journey. He often said he was nearly trauma free, (our family makes films about that kind of stuff) he helped us with our business and had a good understanding of it. Now, this is important, because his dad lost his best friend and so did I at a young age tragically, we as parents, are secretly afraid of losing our kids. We may have been helicopter parents in our days with him.

Taylor didn't have a fear of living any second. No hang ups, he just assumed he could do anything, pushed the boundaries of what's possible and didn't settle. He loved full out and gave the best hugs, his smile made us smile and his laugh was joyous. He played all sports with pure conviction (soccer, weightlifting, road biking, mountain biking, skiing, surfing, swimming, running). He climbed volcanoes in Hawaii and surfed during a hurricane, taught himself the guitar, solved the Rubix Cube in record time, played videos games competitively, created connections everyplace he was, scored a 31 on his pre ACT, he was a good student and college bound, built a business and a website and had a YouTube channel when he was seven.

Taylor was an old Soul, full of discipline, business and relationship goals at fifteen we as adults have failed to accomplish. His desire for self improvement was driven by a Spirit inside of him living to the fullest each day. Taylor had great taste in music.

Did he have insecurities as a deeply layered over thinker? Of course, it was part of his driving force to always go the extra miles when others gave up, although he would try to drag them along telling them they could do it if he could. With the incredible impact Taylor Jennings has had on so many, may his legacy be the extra mile you try as you are afraid and still do it, the can do attitude of thinking you aren't good enough to be empowered to live the life you want and the work ethic of a savage to accomplish the goals you have put off for too long.

See, life is time, it's the only measurable thing we have to our lives and we are given a finite number of minutes to be our best in this meat suit that carries us through earth life.

Today, as his body is put to final rest and some of you may have a chance to have some closure in person as your grieving begins, please know, he's not there, he is with you when you smile, laugh and have admiration for yourself as a good person doing their best in this earth school that continues to give you opportunities to make an impact helping others to be their best. Our mourning is for us, not him, as we feel our expectation of that potential loss.

I am sending strength, peace and love as his mother to everyone today including his father, Andrew Jennings, my mom Dawn Carlson, Brian, Morgan & Ashlee Ross, Kevin, Devon, Kobe, Lauren, Cody and Raelyn Carlson, his girlfriend Lexi Radtke and her family, Tanner Barse, Ann Rutta, Tim, Ben, Pete Jennings, their spouses and his 13 cousins, all of his sports family, coaches and fans. Peace be with you on your journey.

In the book of life, the chapter on Grief
is really all about Love.

–Sandy Walden, Grief Coach, Author

Remembering Taylor

With the pandemic surrounding us, I started thinking I had the coronavirus. My chest hurt bad, and I was short of breath. Catching the virus would have been preferable to experiencing what I realized were the psychosomatic effects of my sadness and trauma. My body felt challenged and fatigued.

I am a quick processor and executor of information. These traits have given me an edge most of my life. After Taylor's death, I had no edge, no advantage, no guru inside of me leading the way. I was alone inside my thoughts. My body ached everywhere. I couldn't process them quickly, so I just sat with it, accepted this way of being for now, leaned into the pain, and prayed it would pass through me in the next few days. Maybe then I would want to shower, eat, or even look at someone without being angry or crying inconsolably.

On day four, I finally remembered that I had all of the tools in my rational state. In my recent past, I had served as a Shaman, helping others through their trauma. But where was my inner medicine woman now? She seemingly checked out when I needed her most. I could not access all my knowledge and implement it for myself. I just cried and felt helpless, like a four-year old whose puppy just got run over by a car in front of her. Ughhhh!

That night Taylor visited me unexpectedly. I felt his presence and heard him say, "I love you, Mom." That was a confidence booster for sure. I remember smiling, and my body feeling his energy. It felt familiar and that was a great way to be sent to sleep.

A couple days later, I was sleeping through each night and that was super helpful for me to continue to process this trauma. My mind was working overtime to put things where they needed to be. This allowed me to find some comfort in the familiar, the things I did every day.

Beginning on day 6, I started to eat regularly and that helped too. More important, I began talking with my family daily. I found it powerful to say Taylor's name and include him in the conversations because he still felt here. I can feel him and sometimes hear him laugh with us when we are being grateful or just being dorks. His funny nuances are burned into my memory thankfully.

I think it's important to allow the healing process and to know that if you miss someone who has died it's okay to live your life. Sure, it's going to be a different version of yourself, it will never be the same. It can't be. I'm different now. Realizing that is a good first step. Acknowledging this change and accepting it is key. Only then can you very slowly craft a plan, sometimes hour by hour, to find strength to love your new reality.

> Grief comes in heavy like a big wave. It takes you from being okay. And then while trying to maintain, a reminder hits you and that heaviness comes back. Grief is a multistage process that takes time to heal.
>
> –Brian Ross, filmmaker, author

Brian Shares His Grief

April 20, 2020 journal entry

This is my first journal entry since Taylor's unexpected passing. I really haven't been ready to write about it yet. My focus has been only on Kimberly and the kids. This is literally the hardest thing a family will ever go through, and I don't know how this will go. I have been praying a lot for God to put his hand of love on Kimberly, Andrew, and the rest of the family. If I am honest with myself, I didn't want to accept the truth myself about losing him. I am not his biological dad. He has a great dad in Wisconsin. I am just his mentor and part time dad when he came to visit us at our home in Florida. That being said, I have grown to really love the little guy over the last 3 years. We kind of thought that he would eventually move in with us as he got older. He stayed with us during summer break and Christmas breaks and long weekends.

I love my two daughters dearly however, I never had a son and now I had two with Zach and Taylor. The last several days have been a roller coaster ride delivered like a crushing blow from hell. I am constantly thinking how could this have happened? With everything else happening in the world there's a part of me that is considering whether there is some strange possibility that we have shifted to an alternate reality or dimension. Nothing is right. Then I walk by my studio and I notice Kim is in there working?

How is that possible? How is she doing that? I was just holding her while she sobbed in desperation 10 minutes ago.

I am struggling with my own emotions. I am angry at Taylor one minute for doing something to put himself at risk then crying in sadness at the reality of it all. He believed he was unstoppable and he really was. How could this have happened? God, I love my daughters so much but Taylor was like a son I never had. He had so many plans to do things. I love his energy and his can do attitude. Every time I walk outside I see his car we just bought him. He was only 15 but his 16th birthday was coming soon and we wanted to surprise him with it when he came down to stay with us.

I am really concerned about my oldest daughter Morgan. She really took Taylor's death hard. They became so close, like brother and sister. She thinks she was at fault for Taylor's drowning. Kim and I keep talking to her about it and letting her know that she was not to blame and to please try to let those feelings go. Fortunately, the kids are getting therapy and it's helping somewhat.

I am feeling super melancholy today. This feeling came over me that I couldn't shake. I went for a bike ride, worked out and even worked in the garden planting flowers and trimming the bamboo I planted in Taylor's name but I couldn't move through it. I keep seeing this vision of

Taylor on the ground next to the pool every time I walk by the pool. I have been pretty much keeping that to myself because I don't want to freak everyone out.

My heart feels broken when I think about Kim doing CPR with me on Taylor!!! That should never happen to a mom. Especially my best friend Kim. God this is so hard to wrap my arms around.

It's a new day! Kim has this strange way of seeming like nothing happened and business as usual. Wait, I spoke too soon and she was crying again. Damn this is beyond difficult and we have so much to do. Saturday night comes and Andrew, Taylor's dad, calls and Kim talks to him for 2.5 hours. It sounded like it was an upbeat conversation which is good. It's Sunday now and I am feeling pretty good. Ok, today is going to be better and then Taylor's dad Andrew calls again and he is sobbing over pictures he's looking at of Taylor. The day goes by with a feeling of sort of a lucid dream or altered reality at times as we all try to stay busy and happy while not thinking about the continued reality that Taylor is not with us anymore. Bedtime comes and I am getting ready for bed thinking, wow, Kim really is doing great this weekend. We have been talking about processes to move more rapidly and efficiently through the five steps of the grieving process so we can focus more on finding "meaning" - the sixth stage of grief. This is great.

We are feeling good and can't wait to make a video about this. As I come to give Kim a hug and ask her to make sure she goes to bed at a reasonable time so we are rested for the next day, she is glued to her phone looking through all her pictures. I begin to warn her that it's a numbers game and that eventually the sadness will come in and wash her away if she is not careful. I again remind her to get some sleep, but nope, she keeps at it like she always does and everything eventually goes dark and sad for a few hours. Here's the hard part. The next morning in my opinion, Kim is bouncing back from this like nothing happened and has extra energy this morning. When I get back from taking the dogs out, a bike ride and some weight lifting in the garage, in her coping process she is on another mission to complete 100 things and I can't keep up. I am frustrated and still sad from last night and she is onto the next thing. We are grieving differently.

Fortunately, I regain my composure and we agree to film a "state of the union" video letting people know how we've been doing for the last three weeks since this tragedy and what we're doing in the near future with Conscious Content, our media company. After releasing that, we both feel better and hopefully we have an uneventful, less emotional evening and a productive day tomorrow.

April 21, 2020 journal entry

Day by day. We had a really productive day yesterday. Each day seems to get better. The negative feelings come in waves when you least expect it. Kim has been doing really well under the circumstances. She only occasionally loses her mind for short bursts and lashes out at me. I take it with a grain of salt. We have a solid relationship on all fronts and this is difficult at best.

I worked outside all day today getting the irrigation installed to water the bamboo garden I created out back in Taylor's name.

Last night, Kim had an intense spiritual experience with her son Taylor. She said she helped him cross over. He seemed to be stuck in between dimensions. I have read that can happen with accidental deaths. We have both been feeling a lot of heaviness and pressure on us, but I have not been able to connect with him since my very brief experience right after the event. I miss him so much I can't really even talk about him like Kim seems to be able to do. Death is so final. RIP Taylor. I love you little buddy.

Kimberly Shares More Posts Regarding Taylor

May 15, 2020

Day 50 Reminder: life is delicate, such a privilege and many times requires us to take the deepest dive to reach our potential. Time is the only thing we don't get more of.

So we play full out even if we have no idea if it will work out.

I miss you kid, this is the hardest and so many of us miss your energy. It's unlike anything I have ever felt before and you know I don't lose well. We are leaving a legacy and yours will be remembered. You are our fuel and purpose. You were such a tiny human born at 35 weeks barely 5 lbs determined to live against the odds growing into a total badass with the biggest heart. Thank you for your contribution to humanity. I am proud of you. Watch over your brothers!

June 11, 2020

Day 77: Mornings are mostly tough and emotional for me since Taylor died. It's the dreamlike to the reality transition process that sets in. I am moving through the relentless grieving process documenting all of these nuances for a book, paying close attention to each subtlety, feeling it in my body and letting it pass. I have never been a person to numb myself for any reason. I lean in no matter what. Especially when it sucks. The faster I can move it through me, the better.

Today, I reminded myself to stay present and experience nature and watch my puppies appreciate everything as they stay present like a meditation discovering every detail. These are my pictures minutes after waking up moving through what I just described.

Today's lesson: I appreciate my line of site with gratitude. These are some of the things I saw today within my bubble here. Taylor loved it here so much and had Marlon take pictures of him here two days before he left us. I did the same thing 24 hours before. Its diverse, bright, colorful leaves and buds feel like a fairy garden you drop into, a labyrinth you can walk along the paths underneath the Roebelenii palms.

Brian Ross planted four strong bamboo in his honor that are growing like he was. Their tenacity to grow quickly and immense strength remind me of him daily.

June 26, 2020

Hope is alive!! We need it to live in purpose and conviction. Today is 3 months that Taylor, my 15 year old, passed unexpectedly. We were in the middle of our film and book creation and he was so excited and proud of what we were doing to help people. He often sympathized with others about their trauma and wanted to help, but readily admitted he hadn't experienced any of his own. It's the most unsettling and unreal feeling to be educating about PTSD, grief and trauma to the public and experience it in real time. Life is stranger than fiction I assure you. There is no place to hide for me, I chose a public forum in film and media as my business. I just have to work with it the best I can in my uncomfortable, cumbersome human way and give myself grace in the process. I asked for an authentic life and it seems I am given experiences to embrace that narrative no matter how tragic. Mental wellness has never been more vital to everyone's survival as it is right now. We are living an unprecedented history with so much pain and the need for historical acknowledgments we aren't ready to accept. Secrets are being unearthed, clarity in all forms are being delivered globally. It's just so EXTRA, sometimes it's just too much!

Time can lessen the hurt; the empty place we have can seem smaller as other things and experiences fill our life; we can forget for periods and feel as if our loved one didn't die; we can find sense in the death and understand that perhaps this death does fit into a bigger design in the world; we can learn to remember the good and hold on to that.

But we cannot "get over it," because to get over it would mean we were not changed by the experience. It would mean we did not grow by the experience. It would mean that our loved one's death made no difference in our life.

There is an interesting discussion in the Talmud, an ancient Jewish writing. Those Jews had the custom of rending their garments—literally tearing their clothes—to symbolize the ripping apart that death brings. But the question was raised, after the period of mourning, could you sew the garment up and use it again? The teachers answered yes, but when you mended it, you should not tuck the edges under so it would look as if it had never been torn. This symbolized the fact that life after grief is not the same as before. The rent will show.

–Deborah Spungen, author *And I Don't Want to Live This Life: A Mother's Story of Her Daughter's Murder* [42]

July 11, 2020

Happy 22nd BirthDay, Zachary. We smile today, however, the last 365 days of your 21st year were challenging, to say the least.

Our Learnings

✔ To Love the hardest is best

✔ Life is short

✔ Be open to change

✔ Get therapy

✔ Raise your standard to remarkable

✔ Attainment of goals has never been more available with work and dedication

✔ Every second of breathing is a gift

✔ Family first

✔ We are capable of everything we invest in

✔ Resilience is a super power

✔ We rise after the greatest loss

✔ Time helps us to heal

✔ People and my past do not define me

✔ I grow daily from my experiences

✔ I am a better human than I was last year

✔ I am learning to be gentle with myself

Photo of Taylor taken in February 2020.
Photo Credit: Tanner Barse

July 20, 2020

Day 117: When an energy goes back to Source it knows innately the path to go unless there are obstacles or there is an immediate transfer from Body matter to only Lightbody energy (accidental death). Time isn't linear and in a blink of an eye your soul is in a new experience. Those of us left in this dense gravity hurling the earth at 1100 mph feel like it will be forever before we see our loved ones again. Those that have evolved have referred to the time in our physical body as a "3 second life" and they aren't really as "far" away as we think they are.

A different dimension, a different frequency that our basic senses can't feel unless we lift our frequency to theirs. In this higher frequency we are Omnipresent and vibrating so high as Taylor has conveyed to us seemingly in all of the places at once, only a breath away. This image is a picture of him taken by one of his friends I found in his phone from Feb 2020 and is figuratively how I found him three weeks after he passed (April 15th) suspended in a spirit plane, seemingly waiting but not sure for what. This interaction with him was profound to me not only as a Shaman presented with this opportunity to assist once again but as his life-giver this time around. He whispered to me while I was putting clothes away in my walk in closet. I fell to my knees and listened for a moment in disbelief.

I was the last family member to touch him after performing CPR with Brian. Once the transmission was secure, We discussed the previous "haunting" from him with all of us including my mother and why that was happening those past 21 days. He offered up verbal communication, passwords, signs, music and physical experiences to each of us over this time not having realized the consequences of his actions. The dogs were going crazy at multiple households.

We discussed his partial energy matter suspension and he verified he had memory of the drowning accident following his unconsciousness from his "Wim Hof" breathing technique on the inside ledge of the deep side of the pool and underwater, there was no struggle, calming peace, literally an out of body experience.

Evaluating where he was from my perception, we discovered he was presented with the lesson of "guilt," a large dark entity blocking his path and we had to clear it by acknowledging that he didn't have to take it with him to the next stop. Let's call it a karma clearing experience. This lesson was actually holding him in this "place" and in his limited knowledge of his new space thought that this was "it," where he belonged. He was able to dissolve it with direction and the energy of Arch-Angel Michael's blue light ray.

Once this path was cleared, in the distance he witnessed his grandfather, step grandmother, great grandmother, great aunt, and our dog from when he was little to greet him. His hesitation was evident as he didn't want to leave me or our interaction until "Wicker," our griffin who passed several years ago ran to him and urged him to follow him. Anyone who knew Taylor knew he was smitten by animals and their energy would captivate him.

We often say "we don't know what we don't know," in this case it was the same, he thought that placement was it and for such a bright light this was devastating for me to witness. As a Shaman and as my lineage (mother, grandmother, children, etc.), have committed by oath to humanity and the spiritual planes to assist those in need of crossing to their correct astral plane if we feel them or are called. Many can attest to the benefit of those who are still here on the earth plane that have shared space with me during this intimate spiritual experience over the last twelve years. It can be life changing for those left in the physical realm, a huge weight lifts and we can relax knowing "more" than we did before. A sacred contract is fulfilled each time. To those of you who don't know what that means or haven't experienced it, maybe someday you will.

As all of these strange phenomena continue to present themselves these days and seemingly anything positive or negative is possible, the veil wears thin and we are either woke or we are in denial. I was honored to experience Taylor being escorted to his correct astral plane with care and his lesson to acknowledge and clear guilt this time around. This was accomplished and then he was gone, merely contracting and then expanding seemingly everywhere. I haven't felt him physically since. I think of him sometimes minute by minute praying for his peace, laughing at thousands of videos/images he left us. He was an avid documenter.

Since all of our belief systems are being challenged as we speak in the world, I don't feel out of line to say I feel he incarnated already and is on a new journey, this explaining his lack of linger, a clean break in the matrix. His footprint of energy is left for so many to remember. It's painful and remarkable and gives me Opportunity for continued grace with this devastating lesson this time around.

During all of the turbulence you are experiencing in a world of uncertainty, please consider to recognize and internalize your very limited time here in this space we share together. This physical experience you have come to know is just a fraction of who you are as a powerful whole. May grace present itself to you daily and may peace find you as a friendly place to resonate.

Grief Stories from Others

Grief changes us, that's true. Just as every wave changes the sea. We evolve, heal and transform. Life can be beautiful once again.

–Sandy Walden, grief coach, author

We all have stories of grief and loss and we thought you'd like to hear from several others who have struggled and inspired others as a result.

When the Teacher Becomes the Student

Sandy Walden is a master grief coach, Reiki master/ teacher, hypnotist, and author of *The Acorn Journal: Messages of Connection from The Other Side . . . One Acorn at a Time*. Sandy always thought of herself as a wife and mom first. When she learned that her youngest son, Mike, had taken his own life at the age of twenty-three, she learned firsthand what it was like to be plunged into deep grief.

Sandy was very aware that while she was indeed experiencing deep, complicated grief, she was not dealing with PTSD because of the suicide and neither were her family members. For every person, grief is totally and completely unique. Some people will experience PTSD symptoms.

Turning to books, her number one go-to when facing a new situation, Sandy was horrified to read again and again that most marriages crumble after losing a child to suicide and that all surviving members were at heightened risk of taking their own lives in the months after this loss. Book after book, website after website, delivered the message that this pain of losing someone to suicide would be with her for the remainder of her life.

Listening to her intuition and with a rather stubborn bit of determination, she knew this could not, would not, be her truth nor would it be the truth for her husband and surviving sons. They would survive. They would heal. They would once again thrive. And they would indeed bring the love that they carried for Mike along with them for the remainder of their lives.

The tools that Sandy had in her professional box—including coaching, Reiki, hypnosis, and more—served her well as she listened to her intuition and trusted Spirit to guide her.

Determination and hope went hand in hand with the deliberate choice to find a way to heal. For Sandy, this meant finding a safe, healthy way to express what she was thinking and feeling. Unable to find face-to-face support groups in her area, she turned to the Internet and after several weeks stumbled across Alliance of Hope for Suicide Loss Survivors (AOH). As she sat down to read, she began to feel as though perhaps she wasn't the only person who felt the Earth should have stopped spinning. She realized that she wasn't alone. Others understood. And she began to breathe again.

Within a short time, Sandy began telling her story. She realized that while she was often the strong support for immediate family and friends, she needed an outlet where she could be totally vulnerable. The forum within this website provided this outlet, and her healing began.

Sandy began working behind the scenes for AOH as well as supporting those who were just beginning their journey. She learned on a new and very personal level how deeply healing it is to reach out and support others. It helped her to be very aware that her healing was happening while showing her that she still mattered to the world at large. She had a purpose. She mattered.

Sandy participated in the forum at AOH for several years. She volunteered for well over forty hours a week as a moderator and mentor as well as continuing behind the scenes projects.

These days, Sandy focuses primarily on supporting those who are grieving a death. She adamantly pushes back against the oft-repeated proclamation that one must suffer for the rest of their lives because grief can never heal. When someone tells her they must live the remainder of their life in pain, she simply asks them why that must be true.

While your truth may be similar to someone else's, it may also be very different. Listen to experts, consider advice that is given by others, but listen to your inner guidance, to your own heart.

More than anything, Sandy encourages you to remember that you have the choice to heal. It won't happen in an instant. It won't happen overnight. But if you are willing to do the work, to experience and move through the hurt and pain, healing will begin. (See The Wisdom Well for Sandy's contact information.)

Tiffany Anderson's Story of Grief and Loss

I lost my dad when I was thirteen. My dad had kidney failure due to complications from when he was younger.

That was kind of a hard transition, being young and losing my dad. In April of 2015, my mom went into the hospital. She was having stomach pains and we found out she had a minor stroke after they did iodine testing. Her kidneys were shutting down and for a good portion of the time she was sedated in the hospital. She passed away on June 7, 2015. Dealing with that transition was really hard because we had never really seen my mom sick. It was tough for my siblings as well. There are five of us total, and she had two grandchildren at the time.

I was thirty and my thirty-first birthday was in August. Knowing that was my first birthday without my mom was difficult simply because usually at midnight, she's the first person to call me. She's the first person to wish me a happy birthday. And so it was just hard. I had a lot of friends that were in town though because I had planned to do a photo shoot for my birthday and everyone had already taken the time off for that birthday photo shoot. They kept me occupied and made sure we laughed and had fun. So, my friends really made that first birthday after losing my mom memorable for me. After they left, it got tough to imagine future birthdays. You see, my mom did a lot of things for us kids for our birthdays and making sure we knew we were special. I wasn't ready to lose her at that age. She was our biggest supporter.

Realizing that she wouldn't be there for other big life events like me having my first child or me getting married and things like that was kind of difficult. As a result, I turned to alcohol. It became my BFF. I didn't know how to cope without her. I talked to her nearly every day. At the time, I worked at a busy call center in customer service. I was right back to work the Monday following her services. I had no time to grieve.

Often, I'd just have to tell my supervisor I needed to leave work early. I just wanted to numb myself to all the thoughts and confusion going through my head. Drinking alcohol allowed me to suppress all my thoughts and helped me go to sleep without having to face reality or the world. Soon, alcohol became my morning coffee or tea. It was my lunchtime drink and I stopped for more on the way home.

I had lost other people and family members like my dad, but this was different. When I was younger, I wasn't taught the right coping mechanisms or how to grieve properly, so I just kind of buried the stuff and kept it moving in the best way I knew how. As an adult, I had access to different things that helped to numb me from the realities of life—alcohol. Then, in August 2015, I lost my cousin to breast cancer. A month later I was let go from my job because mentally, I wasn't there. In October 2015, I lost my uncle, my dad's brother. Then, in January 2016, I lost my best friend from high school. During a pregnancy, her hormones activated a brain tumor that was dormant.

I was like, I don't know how to maneuver through all of this without my mom. At one time, I would have reached for the church. But, I kind of pulled away from church after I lost my mom because that was one of the things that we did together. My mother was a missionary and I was in the choir. We also did a lot of cooking for the church together.

After losing my job, I realized I was a borderline alcoholic and then ended up losing my apartment because I wasn't working and couldn't pay rent. I didn't know what to do. Normally, I would call my mother knowing she'd be there for me. But, I no longer had that option. I asked myself, "What the hell is going on in my life?" I moved in with a friend and then he lost his place. At this point I was homeless, living out of my car bouncing from couch to couch and staying with my siblings, but I didn't want to be a burden to them. So, I wouldn't stay very long. Finally, I found a job and started doing Uber and Lyft to make extra money which allowed me to move into a new apartment in 2017.

What helps me deal with my grief/PTSD?

My mom was a very creative person who loved to paint, cook, and also was a seamstress. So, I use art as a creative outlet. I love to paint using acrylics. In 2018, I started gardening. My gardening instincts have been passed down by my grandmother. But, I was still struggling and since I wasn't drinking alcohol, I started smoking marijuana to escape reality. In November 2018, I had something they call a marijuana-induced mental breakdown. It forced me to face a lot of the stuff. I actually admitted myself to a mental health hospital because I felt like I was having hallucinations. It was just a lot. I was so scared. They basically told me my breakdown was caused by not dealing with my grief properly. Basically, my grief just boiled over. They recommended intensive therapy for me. The first thing my therapist asked me was, "Do you have a pet? Do you have plants?" My response was no. I asked why it mattered. She said I needed something to take care of.

Ray of Light

In those deepest moments of pain, have a conversation with the person you're grieving over. Talk to them, or perhaps write them a letter. Tell them what you are thinking and feeling. If you're angry, let them know. Go ahead and tell them that you made their favorite dinner and thought about them. Imagine them sitting with you, or walking by your side. Express what is in your heart. And then close your eyes and listen with your magnificent heart. They are reaching back to you, sending you so much love. Remember, always remember, the love never dies.

Fishing in the Wisdom Well

Add some plants to your environment, either in your house or outside. Why do it? Indoor and outdoor green spaces improve well-being. Texas A&M University researchers confirmed that living in or near green spaces and spending as much time as possible in natural settings and cultivated gardens can improve mood, reduce stress, and encourage more physical activity. Other benefits include better cognition and less aggression in people of all ages.[43]

On the advice of my therapist, I got a few plants and started to learn a lot of life lessons from my plants. Someone once told me that my relationship with my plants can relate to my relationship with my mom. We didn't have the opportunity to fully make our relationship the best it could be as sometimes we struggled with communication. There were a lot of things I would not tell my mom about. So, this was something we were working on. I started paying attention to the way my plants were and how they were growing. Maybe this plant needed a lot of sun and this one needed water. I kind of learned how my mom was able to be a parent to us kids through my plants. Some of the plants need a little more watering than others and some of the other plants are a little wilder than others. Discovering this kind of helped to heal me and process some of that grief. The biggest part of grief is recognizing you're grieving.[44]

As of this writing, Tiffany is working on her Phat Girl Chronicles podcast, where she focuses on life, fashion, and what it means to be a sassy phat girl in today's world.

There's a Sixth Stage of Grief

In grief and trauma, we often feel so isolated. The world seems to be moving on and does not recognize that we are in such a different place. We may look fine on the outside, what's happening on the inside is a different story.

–David Kessler, grief specialist and author

Right before she died in 2004, Elisabeth Kübler-Ross collaborated with David Kessler for her final book, *On Grief and Grieving*, where they introduced the sixth stage of grief, which is finding meaning in grief. In 2019, he wrote a book, *Finding Meaning: The Sixth Stage of Grief*.

In this book, Kessler gives readers a roadmap to remembering those who have died with more love than pain; he shows us how to move forward in a way that honors our loved ones. Kessler's insight is both professional and intensely personal. His journey with grief began when, as a child, he witnessed a mass shooting at the same time his mother was dying. For most of his life, Kessler has taught physicians, nurses, counselors, and first responders about end-of-life trauma and grief and has led talks and retreats for those experiencing grief. Despite his knowledge, his life was again upended by the sudden death of his twenty-one-year-old son.

How does a grief expert handle such a tragic loss? He knew he had to find a way through this unexpected, devastating loss, a way that would honor his son. That, ultimately, was the sixth stage of grief—meaning. And this is what we are trying to do with Taylor's death—create meaning of it even while we are going through this.

Grief Affects Your Body and Mind

As we said at the beginning of this chapter, grief is messy—real messy. And it's real. Medical doctors classify grief into two categories: acute and persistent. The majority of people experience acute grief, which occurs in the first six to twelve months after a loss and gradually resolves. Persistent grief lasts longer than twelve months.

With acute grief, thoughts and memories can make it difficult to accept the loss. Chronic stress also is common during acute grief and can lead to a variety of physical and emotional issues, such as depression, trouble sleeping, feelings of anger and bitterness, anxiety, loss of appetite, and general aches and pains.

People who experience persistent grief should seek out a therapist or counselor to help them work through the grieving process. This may include focused treatments such as cognitive behavioral therapy and complicated grief therapy. As with PTSD, having hope is something that can make a big difference with your grief and help you find that meaning.

Ray of Light

There are days when the fog of grief is heavy and the way forward may feel hidden. There are times, moments, days, or sometimes longer when overwhelm visits. This may be prompted by a day of significance or just a tough day. Here are some suggestions on what you can do to get past this:

Take a few deep . . . slow . . . calming . . . breaths.
When we take those deep breaths, it slows down our heart and our mind follows. Even if it's for a short time, we get that respite. The more we practice, the more natural and easy it comes to us.

Have a plan.
Having that plan reminds us that we have a measure of control. It may be small, but it's something, and when we are grieving a loss it often feels that much of life is out of our control. What might that plan look like?

- Ask a friend or companion to be beside you during a difficult time.
- Rehearse saying your loved one's name out loud.
- Call someone who can listen with support and compassion.

Many find it helpful to map out the day or break it down to much smaller, more manageable portions of time—the afternoon, an hour, or even the next few minutes.

Know that it's alright to feel however you feel.
There is no need to judge your feelings. Emotions are gauges that indicate what is happening within. You might feel sad, nostalgic, joyful, or something else. There are absolutely no rules that say you must feel a specific way as you move through grief. As you accept your feelings, you are more easily able to process and move through them or embrace and expand them if they feel good for you.

Take a bit of exercise.
It may be a walk or run outside, yoga, stretching, lifting weights, or something different. It's really about what feels good for you. Moving the body helps to move our thoughts, which can shift our perspective and release those endorphins.

Do something kind or thoughtful for someone else.
It may seem counterintuitive when we are struggling to reach out to another to offer kindness or support, but it's powerful. It reminds us that we matter and that we can make a difference in the world that matters. Research shows that each time we do something for another, whether it be a gesture or even a loving word, our serotonin levels rise. This is even more of a win-win than you might imagine. We benefit, the one who we reach out to benefits, and even those who witness or hear about the kindness experience a rise in serotonin.[55]

As you walk this path, through grief and into healing,
please know that you are not alone.

–Sandy Walden, grief coach, author

It's time to take a sip from The Wisdom Well.

Note all the resources listed here can be accessed on https://Consciouscontent.org by clicking on the Wisdom Well Resources link.

THE WISDOM WELL

Reading:

Kessler, David. *Finding Meaning: The Sixth Stage of Grief.* NY: Scribner, 2019. In this groundbreaking new work, David Kessler—an expert on grief and the coauthor with Elisabeth Kübler-Ross of the iconic On Grief and Grieving—journeys beyond the classic five stages to discover a sixth stage: meaning.

Walden, Sandy. *The Acorn Journal: Messages of Connection from the Other Side.* (Sandy Walden: 2019). When someone we love has died, we miss them. We wonder where they are now. Are they alright? Can they see and hear us or are we disconnected forever? We long for a sign that death is not the end; that someday we will meet again. After the devastating loss of their youngest son to suicide, the Walden's had these same thoughts and questions. This book is about the confirmation they received in a most joyful way. It is full of love and hope and needs to be read by everybody who has lost a loved one.

Hairston, Stephanie. How Grief Shows Up in Your Body. WebMD. Looks at the difference between normal grief and pathological grief and how it harms our bodies, especially our immune systems.

The creator of the Way for Hope website, Jan McDaniel is a suicide loss survivor. She is also a journalist and author.

Ronnie Walker created Alliance of Hope to support others after the loss of her stepson to suicide.

Dietmar, Kramer. *New Bach Flower Therapies Healing the Emotional and Spiritual Causes of Illness.* Rochester, VT: Healing Arts Press, 1995. Bach Flower Remedies are timeless. Created by Dr. Edward Bach (1886-1936), his pioneering research and essences have found a permanent place in homeopathic medicine for uplifting and shifting emotional states. Dr. Bach treated the whole person, and saw dis-ease as an effect of disharmony between the mind, body and soul. Naturopath Dietmar Kramer has built upon Bach's foundation, identifying uses for healing emotional states related to external influences along with deep-rooted internal emotional conflicts.

Watching/Listening:

David Kessler shares the best Movies About Grief along with short descriptions of each and how they could be helpful to someone experiencing a specific type of grief.

Unlocking Us with Brené Brown: "David Kessler and Brené on Grief and Finding Meaning" (45:14) Brene and David talk about why he added the sixth stage of grief—the meaning of grief to the Elisabeth Kübler-Ross' five stages of grief, which are: denial, anger, bargaining, depression, and acceptance.

Phat Girl Chronicles, a podcast by Tiffany Anderson. Listen to her podcast about life, fashion, love, and living life as a Phat Girl on any of the major podcast platforms, including Spotify.

David Kessler on Why We Become So Fearful on Death and the Importance of Grief. (12:47) A Larry King interview where he shared his book *Finding Meaning: The Sixth Stage of Grief* and explains that as a society we have become more fearful of death than ever before. Plus, why he decided to study death and grieving in the first place.

Coach Bob Bowman and Olympic Swimmer Michael Phelps educate swimmers on the dangers of shallow water blackout and how to prevent it. (3:33)

Dr. Sanjay Gupta warns about shallow water blackout, which puts even the most fit athletes in danger. (4:45)

Taking Action:

Ascension Cards—These cards may be employed in a variety of ways — such as a daily source of guidance and inspiration, a point of study for a group discussion, a source for determining which areas of an ascension path require the most immediate attention.

Grief.com Facebook page. Share your grief with others while gaining support from others and subject matter experts. Join Grief.com. An incredible resource by author and speaker David Kessler. Find a grief support group, find a book on grief, and learn about the different types of grief.

To learn more about Sandy Walden, visit www.Sandy Walden.com. To find additional support, visit her private Facebook group: From Grief to Healing, Rebuilding Relationships with those in the Afterlife.

PART III

#liftthestigma

It's time to lift this stigma and talk about it so the
people suffering can get the help they need.

-Brian Ross

The hardest thing about having PTSD is you can't see it.
When you see someone in a wheelchair,
you know they're disabled.
When you see someone who is blind
with a seeing-eye dog,
you know they're disabled.
But, you don't see post-traumatic stress.

–Nikki Smith, PTSD survivor

Not Enough Conversation

Not enough people are talking about what it means to have a mental breakdown, a mental disorder, or a mental moment where we just don't feel ourselves. We're not saying it's an illness. We're not even saying it's a disorder at this point, but it is an experience that we as human beings are navigating on a regular basis day-to-day, hour-to-hour, and sometimes minute-by-minute, depending on what we've been exposed to.

Stigma and Shame Surrounding Suicide Death

Sandy Walden, grief coach and author tells her story

When my son, Mike, died by his own hand in December of 2010, I expected there to be a stigma. It's unfortunately all too common for those left behind to feel shame about how their loved one died. At the same time, I've always been rather direct and I knew from the very first moment that the way Mike died was simply the door he walked through to get to The Other Side. Because of this I never shied away from the word "suicide." To be honest, I may have been a bit defiant about it, as I felt it was so important that my surviving sons and my husband deserved to be protected from this... as though I had that ability.

The responses of others when they were told how Mike died were often fascinating. It wasn't at all unusual for them to recoil as though they had been struck. They were simply shocked and horrified and were responding quite naturally. I didn't feel stigma or shame around these responses, although I know very well that many who are left behind feel these responses as though they are blows to the gut. I was fortunate that they never landed that way to me, they simply felt natural and I understood in my own way that others were doing the best they could with such shocking information.

Where shame and stigma showed up for me was when I would express my thoughts, feelings and experiences, my own way of healing. It was not at all unusual for me to receive various messages that boiled down to "you don't hurt enough, you must not love Mike as much as I love the person I am missing."

Participating within an online community, my comments were sometimes disregarded or diminished by others because I was not spending each day curled up in a ball sobbing and deeply depressed. This is a completely reasonable response to losing someone to suicide. Having said that, it would seem that my default wiring is a bit different. My pain, my sadness, my grief did not show up as someone else expected, so it was dismissed as not being worthy of acknowledgment. My determination to hold on to and honor the joy, frustration, excitement, and all of the other emotions that I had experienced with this amazing being for twenty-three years was most often expressed in story form and deep gratitude. For me that felt right, but it was anathema to many. It was not unusual for me to receive the message that it was not okay to heal, or that one must suffer for the remainder of their life if they truly loved the person they lost.

I experienced similar comments at gatherings because someone might see me smiling or laughing, but they felt themselves tear up when we were together. More than once it was mentioned to me that they didn't understand how I could show up and be okay when it was so very hard for them to see me and not weep for the loss of Mike.

Should I have felt shame that while I experienced profound sadness, it wasn't the place that I stayed all of the time? My default setting was to be happy, to embrace the memories with a very messy mixture of tears, snot, and laughter.

What was very interesting to me was that it seemed quite natural to take a step back with any of these circumstances and realize that we were each operating from what we knew and understood. Doing the best we could while moving through a unique and incredibly emotionally charged experience.

For me, there was no shame in the way my son died. I refused to pick up and own the stigma surrounding suicide for one single moment. While shame and stigma came my way as it related to my way of grieving and healing, it always felt quite natural to deny them the opportunity to live within my heart. They were not mine. They had no place in my life.

For me, I believe that is because I know that Mike is fine! He is more than fine, he's thriving and there is no reason for those of us who will forever love him to suffer endlessly. We are connected. We always have been. We always will be.[45]

We each walk our path through grief and into healing in our own way. This journey is much easier when we can trust that we are supported and loved regardless of how our steps look to others.

The Label of Mental Illness

Dr. John A. King, author, poet, long-time activist, and sexual abuse and trafficking survivor, shares his story:

Post-traumatic stress disorder is labeled a mental illness, and is something that we haven't come to terms with. I remember being in a business meeting and negotiating this particular real estate deal, and one of the guys called me back from the other side and said, "Hey listen, I just want to let you know that so-and-so told me that he's concerned about doing business with you because you've got post-traumatic stress and we need to give you everything or you're just going to go postal." I think to myself, "I'm going to become some crazed killer because the guy's trying to negotiate a real estate deal?" That's the stigma that's attached to PTSD.

Some of the guys I know that have PTSD and some of the most severe cases of it are the most mellow, gentle men that you would ever meet, because they're in control of what they've experienced. It's the stigma attached to mental illness that made me not want to embrace it. I think fundamentally, people are scared of what they don't know. They don't know about mental illness. When you hear that someone is mentally ill, you think that's a crazy person.

Stigma is defined as a mark of disgrace associated with a particular circumstance, quality, or person. Because there is such a stigma attached to mental illness, people don't talk about it and people who suffer from it don't talk about it because they don't want the stigma attached to it. The less people are talking about it, the less that's known about it, then there is more stigma and mystery.

There are a couple conversations that are happening in this space with people wanting to change the name, but a rose by any other name is still a rose. I think we can spend lots of time trying to come up with an acronym that makes us feel special or important, but the basic line is we are dealing with a mental illness, and the only reason we want to change the name is because we want to move away from the taint of having to admit to a mental illness. The problem with that is you're allowing everybody else to define your world. If you allow anyone to define your world, they will define it too small. I just own it.

I am just a little bit crazy. I have demons.
Sometimes we cuddle and sometimes I kick them out.

–Dr. John King

Unscheduled Brain Scan

In 2016, I traveled to a business meeting in Atlanta to connect with some people working with innovative medical technology. It was some new portable brain scan technology that they'd used extensively on pro athletes and on combat vets with post-traumatic stress. I'm sitting around this table with this bunch of guys. One of the guys says, "Hey, anyone want to try this?" They chanted, "Hey, let the Australian try it." I had to sit there and take this test. The doctor operating the system took what looked like a shower cap or a colander that had a bunch of probes hanging off it. He attached the probes to my scalp and the scanner to his laptop. I sat there looking like something from Young Frankenstein. The guys thought it was awesome.

The doctor began the test, and I went through the assessment while everyone else went back to the business at hand. The results come up. The doctor is scrolling through the results and looking at me. The room's quiet. They're waiting for the funny comments. He says, "Okay, I need to see you outside." I follow him out, he says, " I didn't know that you were a veteran."

"I'm not," I said. "I haven't served in the military."

"You must've played as a pro athlete."

"No, I haven't."

"This is the worst case of brain trauma and the changes in the brain that I've ever seen. This is as bad as anything that I've ever witnessed compared to combat veterans."

And that moment was the first time I had empirical proof of the impact of the trauma on my life, on my brain, and the changes that it had made and the physiological changes that had happened.

My frontal lobe was shut down—that's your day-to-day memory and that's your day-to-day response to things. The amygdala, which controls your fight and flight responses, was working overtime because it's trying to compensate for other things. If you can imagine the very thing that's supposed to stop you from responding isn't working and the thing that is saying, "You've got to respond to every-thing!" is working overtime. This explained the panic attacks, the paranoia, and the brain's inability to balance things out. It's why I was so upset by things so readily. It was just fascinating to see how all those things tied together.

If people could understand that PTSD is a fundamental change to your brain and you have to deal with it in a totally different way, it's not the flu, it's not cancer, but it's a change that's going to be with you forever, and it changes your behavior, it changes the fundamentals of who you are, then your approach to healing is different.

You deal with it differently. You have to assess how you will regain or find balance differently. It's a memory filing error. When we have memories, we've got places to put these things, like here's a happy family event, here's graduation. When you have a traumatic event, you don't know where to place that. You can't file it anywhere, so in a sense it just sits like this folder full of papers of memories or photos. It sits there, and on the desk that is our life or our mind, we don't know where to put it. The brain doesn't quite know how to process it in the context of what happens on a day-to-day basis.[46]

PTSD and Your Brain

As we explored trauma brain research more in depth, we discovered Dr. Jennifer Sweeton, who is a licensed clinical psychologist and internationally recognized expert on anxiety and trauma, women's issues, and the neuroscience of mental health. Her credentials are worth noting as she completed her doctoral training at the Stanford University School of Medicine, the Pacific Graduate School of Psychology, and the National Center for PTSD. Additionally, she holds a master's degree in affective neuroscience from Stanford University and studied behavioral genetics at Harvard University.

Dr. Sweeton has written a book entitled *Trauma Treatment Toolbox: 165 Brain-Changing Tips, Tools & Handouts to Move Therapy Forward* to help clinicians treat their clients with

PTSD. What we loved about the book was how it explained how the brain changes when traumatized. While we can't share all of this information here, we'll provide you a few excerpts:

> The amygdala is often hyper-activated when you are suffering from symptoms of PTSD.

> The insula, or the interoception center of your brain, allows you to be aware of, and connect with, all of your internal sensations and experiences. Without a strong and regulated insula, it is very difficult to identify not only physical sensations but also emotions. This is because emotions are always experienced in the body as well as the mind.

> The hippocampus, the memory center of the brain, is responsible for putting a timestamp on our memories. When you have PTSD, the hippocampus often provides inaccurate information to the amygdala. When the amygdala processes sensory information, it asks the question, "Is this dangerous?" To determine whether it is dangerous, it often consults with the hippocampus, asking, "Has this situation/context/person/stimulus ever been dangerous before?" If the hippocampus is not functioning properly, it may respond to the amygdala inaccurately, informing it that a benign situation or stimulus is in fact dangerous.

The prefrontal cortex is considered the thinking center of the brain. This part of the brain is necessary for functioning well in the world and forming relationships with others. If your brain is traumatized, this impacts your ability to concentrate, make decisions, and connect with others. Better self-awareness happens when there is increased activation in this part of the traumatized brain.

The cingulate cortex regulates your emotion and thoughts. Consider this part of the brain as a master control center that attempts to quiet the amygdala and works with the prefrontal cortex to improve decision making and functioning. With people who are suffering from PTSD, when trauma happens, it can cause problems with emotion regulation, thought regulation, good decision making, and judgment.[47]

Understanding the functions of each part of the brain helps explain why people who have PTSD often struggle. Our brains are designed to change throughout life. So it's not unreasonable to expect that an adverse event would adversely affect how the brain gets reprogrammed.

Brain Scans Can Reveal a Lot but Aren't Common

Dr. Daniel Amen is a psychiatrist and founder of Amen Clinics and BrainMD. He advocates for and conducts brain scans on people who are struggling with PTSD, traumatic brain injury, Alzheimer's, and athletes with head injuries, among others. Specifically, he relies on brain SPECT (single-photon emission computed tomography) imaging to diagnose and monitor conditions that affect the health of the brain. Brain scans are helpful for these diagnoses because it assists in determining your best treatment plan.

According to Dr. Amen, SPECT looks at the blood flow and activity of your brain and at how well your brain is functioning. Generally, healthy brains have the most activity in the back of the brain. When comparing a healthy brain to a traumatized brain, there are stark differences. Unhealthy brains literally have holes in them and can look like Swiss cheese. SPECTs aren't commonly performed, however. They aren't typically covered by insurance and need to be paid out of pocket. And they cost around $1,300.

In Dr. Amen's 2011 TEDx Talk, "Change Your Brain, Change Your Life," he exclaimed, "Did you know that psychiatrists are the only medical specialists that virtually never look at the organ they treat? Think about it! Cardiologists look, neurologists, look, orthopedic doctors look, virtually every other medical specialties look—psychiatrists guess. Before imaging, I always felt like I was throwing darts in the dark at my patients." [48]

Dr. Amen views PTSD not as a mental disorder but a brain disorder. SPECT imaging, he believes, proves that PTSD is a biological problem in the brain, not a character flaw or sign of personal weakness.

Note that some in the field of psychiatry find Dr. Amen's use of SPECT imaging controversial. If you are interested in a deeper dive into SPECT and some of the controversy surrounding it and the Amen Clinic, check out some resources at The Wisdom Well.

> SPECT tells you three things about the brain—
> good activity, too little, or too much.
>
> –Daniel Amen, MD

Fishing in the Wisdom Well

How Is an MRI Different from a SPECT Scan?

An MRI is an anatomy study. It shows what the brain physically looks like. SPECT is a nuclear medicine study that looks at blood flow and activity in the brain. It's a functional study. To put it in concrete terms, an MRI shows you what the car engine physically looks like. The SPECT scan shows you how it works when you turn the engine on.

Ray of Light

When feeling overwhelmed, try to relax by breathing. Sit in a quiet and comfortable place. Put one of your hands on your chest and the other on your stomach. Take a slow and regular breath in through your nose. Breathe out through your mouth slowly. Repeat this process at least ten times or until you begin to feel calm.

Retrain Your Brain

Wouldn't it be great if you could retrain your brain? The good news is it is possible. According to Dr. Amen, you are not stuck with the brain you have. Using his brain-smart program, they've demonstrated that 80 percent of people can improve their brains in the areas of blood flow, memory, and mood. Consequently, they can reverse brain damage.

You are braver than you believe,
stronger than you seem and smarter than you think.

–Winnie the Pooh

Brian Ross Reveals What PTSD Looks Like For Him

As an adult, my life looked well put together on the outside. I lived in the right neighborhood, drove the right car, and had great kids, but it all started unraveling while my relationship of nearly thirty years was ending. In the business world, I'd experienced huge financial gains and losses over the years, which led me to reinvent myself multiple times. Even when I was struggling, nobody knew because I was really good at compartmentalizing.

According to the American Psychological Association, compartmentalization is a defense mechanism in which thoughts and feelings that seem to conflict or to be incompatible are isolated from each other in separate and apparently impermeable psychic compartments. It's common in trauma victims.

As I think back, I may have been compartmentalizing since I was a young child. So, when something I determined "bad" happened to me, I would stuff it inside. I never wanted to burden other people with my problems. I felt they wouldn't relate so I kept my feelings to myself.

I was burying my worries and unresolved problems away in these little compartments. I shoved them to the back of my mind, so I could go on pretending they didn't exist.

Eventually, I started to run out of places to put them. Things began to unravel. In 2017, I was fortunate to meet someone through a mutual business partner who had experience in dealing with trauma and had the time and desire to listen. Her name was Kimberly Resch. Speaking to her was the first time I felt comfortable enough to begin talking about what I had experienced. I talked and she listened and offered helpful advice.

Over the next few years, we became quite good friends, although we had never met face to face. Kimberly was just a wonderful voice and a listening ear on the other end of the line. Eventually, after meeting Kimberly in person and spending time with her, I confirmed that putting my feelings away in the wrong place can wreak havoc on my body. I was feeling tired and worn down. I had learned that our body holds those memories, many times ineffectively, and that those memories may cause disease if not filed or released correctly.

I am still realizing that if we perceive ourselves as a collection of these traumas, this baggage will keep us stationary in the past rather than living in the moment. Putting these events in their proper place to be processed so we can move ahead is paramount to recovering from PTSD.

Lifting the Stigma

After enduring many successes followed by tragic failures, there was a point where I felt I couldn't go on. For my sanity, I put experiences in boxes that didn't associate with each other. I intuitively knew this wasn't a sustainable coping mechanism; it did allow me to continue being a functional human.

I knew something had to change. I had to draw a line in the sand and commit to getting some help. But for who? My sanity? My family? Myself? I didn't want to see a psychologist or a psychotherapist. Given my career at the time, if anyone found out, I was sure I would be judged or worse, told I wasn't fit for my responsibilities. The word *stigma* came to mind.

As a man, I understand the stigma of PTSD. Stigma has kept a lot of really great people from seeking help for fear of being judged or labeled as broken. People don't want to go to their medical doctor and get a diagnosis because they feel they'll be identified in the medical system as a psychiatric risk.

The good news is that now there are resources out there for people like you and me. No one has to feel like they're broken or that if they ask for help they will be labeled.

You are not alone and you have value. You can get help and you too can be a light in the darkness. Sometimes we have to be reminded of our worth and that we offer value not only to ourselves, we offer our experience and life lessons to those who are willing to listen.

I know it hurts. I know you feel like you weren't good enough. But your breakthrough is coming. Don't give up on yourself now. You came too far. Your value is still high and you're still beautiful. You don't need anyone to claim you to feel whole. Let it hurt and grow from it.

–Keishorne Scott

Ray of Light

A gentle, two-minute head massage will trigger oxytocin to release. You can massage your own head. Use your fingers to gently massage the scalp, forehead, nose, jaws, and ears. The touch, warmth, and movement release the oxytocin in your brain, lowering your blood pressure and calming your racing thoughts. These brief moments of safe and loving touch give you a few moments' relief from stress and pressure, priming you to cope more resiliently with the next stressor that comes along.

Oxytocin is a powerful hormone often referred to as the "love hormone." It is linked to more social interaction, well-being, and less stress. Besides infant-mother interactions especially during breast feeding, behaviors like hugging, cuddling, having sex, and romantic connection increase oxytocin. Researchers have demonstrated that a single exposure to oxytocin can create a lifelong change in the brain."[49] but to those who are willing to listen.

The Conundrum of PTSD

Usually with an illness, you take medicine and it's gone.
Regarding PTSD, for a lot of people it never ends
or if it does, it's a long process of healing.

–Jennifer Jamison, APSW

Deanna Culver, a PTSD survivor, is an aspiring actor and model, volunteer, photographer, poet, film writer, and an associate producer with a passion for helping people and animals. She believes in bringing awareness and prevention to bullying, suicide, domestic violence, child abuse, animal abuse, mental illness, addiction, and homelessness. Deanna lives with a few disabilities that others may not see or notice but can hinder her day to day. However, she does her best to keep moving forward through the pain she experiences because she's trying to live life to the fullest on the journey she's been traveling. She has experienced physical, emotional, mental, and psychological abuse in and out of the home, school, marriage, workplace, and has conquered addiction to find her way while raising her children and now helping with her grandchildren.

Deanna Culver

My three daughters have been first and foremost in my recovery. Without them and my grandchildren, I definitely wouldn't be here. It's not to say you don't have your moments struggling with living with a mental illness and self-worth. I had my daughters and grandchildren whom I adore and love more than anything, but that didn't stop me from attempting suicide back in 2015. It can be a tremendous struggle at times for anyone. I myself now realize I'm lucky I survived my suicide attempts in the past, but mainly this one in 2015 because I had seconds to survive this attempt.

Now my outlook is different on life as God has definitely opened my eyes to where I understand now that it wouldn't have been good nor fair to my children and grandchildren if I had taken my life away from them and away from myself to enjoy what God has to offer us all. I am here for a reason. So, when I encounter others in their struggles I do my best to help support and guide them on their journey to find their courage and strength to keep moving forward and not give up on themselves.

This is one reason I have published my first book of poetry in 2018. My poetry is a way for me to get my thoughts and feelings out, whether it's anger, frustration, sadness, or happiness, it's a healing mechanism for myself in hopes of also helping others who read it. In turn, writing poetry for me helps alleviate some of the agony or trauma of whatever I'm dealing with at the time.

Before writing my book, I would write my poetry and then put it in a box. I opened my box of poems and determined which ones I wanted to put in my book. As a kid, I wrote poems as a creative outlet too, however, I wasn't allowed to keep anything around. Anything that I considered sacred was tossed or burnt by my mother. So, my poems were written while I was an adult. Some people like journaling. I like writing poems. I just start writing and all of a sudden, my brain goes a different way and I just start rhyming which turn into poems. It's just my way of telling a story and expressing my feelings.

The following is a shortened version of Deanna's poem from her book, *Open Boxed Poetry*:

Living with a Mental Illness

I wish I could understand my own mind
Ups and downs running me blind
I try to wake up from visions of what I wish I
    could be
Why must it be so hard to be normal to be me

I sometimes feel like I'm going out of my mind and
    crazy
Can my body be in this much pain as sometimes I
    feel so lazy
If people only knew the sadness I feel on a daily
    basis
I wish I could run away and find a beautiful oasis
I've been hiding within myself for way to long
Unsure of how to go about help and where I belong

I do nature photography and [turn my pictures] into cards with positive messages. Recently, I mailed out over 100 of my photography cards to thank first responders in hospitals, clinics, police departments, and fire departments as a way of showing my appreciation for all that they do on a daily basis.

I volunteer part-time for nine different organizations. I've been volunteering for over thirty-five years—ever since I was a kid. It's just a part of me. It's my calling or something. It feels extremely good helping so many people, in which I'm always hoping my actions will encourage others to volunteer in their communities as well. Even though I've been through so many horrific and traumatic things, volunteering has a way of opening my heart each and every time.

> Your courage is your strength and
> your strength is your courage.
>
> –Deanna Culver

A few other special things I love in life are photography, nature, and bike rides to keep me grounded. I love when it rains and thunders. I love how it replenishes the earth and smells. Plus, I can go outside and wash my hair too. I'm not really religious, but I believe in God and I'm learning so much including that God does love me and never actually hated me as I thought for so long. I'm so fearful of being my mother. I don't want to be my mother. I will not be my mother. Even though I went through so much horrific and traumatic experiences that have made me who I am, it doesn't define who I am.[50]

Ray of Light

The vagus nerve, loaded with oxytocin receptors, resides in the brain stem. You can locate that region by placing your fingers at the back of your skull, where the top of your neck nestles into the skull. A gentle massage to that part of the neck (you can easily do this yourself) can be a potent trigger for the release of oxytocin, increasing feelings of well-being throughout the day.

Stigma Busting: Keep the Conversation about PTSD Going and Seek Help

The stigma of mental illness keeps a lot of people from seeking help. Lots of people live with the symptoms of PTSD without really knowing that they have PTSD because that diagnosis would be worse in their minds than actually getting the help they need. Internally, we create a stigma within ourselves that, "Oh, I've gone through all these traumatic events, and so I must be broken." It's okay to ask for help. It's okay to have a conversation. It's okay to take a deeper dive into what that looks like. Honestly, it's just okay.

Stigma is wrapped around a decision to go see
my doctor, having that documented and thinking
now I'm labeled in the system. That's part of the problem.
The stigma that has been wrapped around mental health,
PTSD, is slowly starting to lift. Once we have a better
understanding of what is happening within us, we can
strive to become the people we know we can be. It's just a
process of acknowledgement and taking action to heal.

-Brian Ross

The Many Faces of Mental Illness

Humpty Dumpty sat on a wall,
Humpty Dumpty had a great fall.
All the king's horses and all the king's men
Couldn't put Humpty together again.

–English nursery rhyme

In Dr. Janet Seahorn's TEDx Talk, "Understanding PTSD's Effect on the Brain, Body, and Emotions," she brilliantly uses the famous nursery rhyme "Humpty Dumpty" to describe what it looks like for people with PTSD as they struggle to make sense of what happened to them. It's like taking a great fall from a wall and trying to put yourself together again. It becomes extra complicated when you don't realize you took a great fall but feel broken. You might feel brittle, fragile, and one crack away from losing it all.

When we're aware that we feel broken, it's natural to want to make sense of what's happening to us. Most of us self-diagnose, but distinguishing between one disorder and another can be confusing. The American Psychiatric Association's *DSM-5*, the bible for psychiatrists and psychologists when it comes to linking a patient's symptoms with a particular disorder, identifies 265 different diagnoses, many with overlapping symptoms. Even mental health professionals get confused when it comes to putting a label on a set of symptoms.

> People really do believe that ignoring things is going to make it disappear or it's going to make it better, and that's not true. Being aware makes you educated, and being educated allows you to know how to handle certain situations. Being aware of PTSD helps you be better equipped to be that person to help that need.
>
> –Linda Bell, a PTSD survivor.

Many people think they suffer from depression, bipolar disorder, borderline personality disorder, or an eating disorder and leave it at that. But the symptoms of these disorders can also be the subtleties of PTSD—or not.

Heredity, environment, diet, and lifestyle influence whether someone will develop a mental health condition. A stressful job or chaotic home life makes some people more susceptible, as do traumatic life events that impact our brain.

Mental illness is something that happens to us—we don't wake up one morning deciding to be depressed, for instance. So, it's important not to judge yourself but learn and do what you can to get help. Being aware that you suffer from a mental illness can help you to understand yourself better, be kinder to yourself, and take steps to heal.

The National Alliance on Mental Illness has a comprehensive website that describes each of the mental illnesses including symptoms. Visit The Wisdom Well at the conclusion of this chapter to learn more about:

anxiety disorders

attention-deficit hyperactivity disorder

bipolar disorder

borderline personality disorder

depression

dissociative disorders

eating disorders

obsessive-compulsive disorder

Psychosis

PTSD

schizoaffective disorder

schizophrenia[51]

There's no one to blame when it comes to mental illness. For many, recovery is probable and possible.

> My past will either define me or refine me.
> I just chose to allow it to refine me.
> I am not my past. I am my future. I think when we
> allow our past to define us, then we never learn
> from it and we never progress from it.
>
> –Dr. John King

We all carry light inside of us, and when we feel it, we can share that light with others and let them know that their light can shine brighter. We all can be a light in the darkness. Just know it's okay to ask for help and that everyone benefits when you do. You receive the help and they get to give. When you feel stronger, you can return the energy when they need it.

Note that all the resources listed here can be accessed at https://Consciouscontent.org by clicking on the Wisdom Well Resources link.

The Wisdom Well

Reading:

Schwartz, Arielle. *Complex PTSD Workbook: A Mind-Body Approach to Regaining Emotional Control and Becoming Whole Again.* (Berkeley, CA: Althea Press, 2016). People affected by complex PTSD commonly feel as though there is something fundamentally wrong with them that somewhere inside there is a part of them that needs to be fixed. Though untrue, such beliefs can feel extremely real and frightening. This book provides a map to the complicated, and often overwhelming,

terrain of Complex PTSD with author Dr. Schwartz's knowl-
edgeable guidance helping you find your way.

Williams, Mary Beth. *The PTSD Workbook: Simple, Effective Techniques for Overcoming Traumatic Stress Symptoms.*
(Oakland, CA: New Harbinger Publications, 2016). The
authors outline techniques and interventions used by
PTSD experts from around the world to conquer distressing trauma-related symptoms. In this workbook, you'll
learn how to move past the trauma you've experienced
and manage symptoms such as insomnia, anxiety, and
flashbacks.

King, John A. *#Dealwithit: Living Well with PTSD.* (Next
Foundation, 2017). This book is the honest, raw, not-safe-for-
work account of Dr. John A. King trying to piece his life back
together, move forward and thrive after the spontaneous
recall of over a decade of childhood sexual abuse by his parents and their friends.

Why is Daniel Amen's Method for Treating Psychiatric
Disorders so Controversial? In this Psychotherapy Net-
worker blog, Mary Sykes Wylie looks at the controversy
behind Dr. Daniel Amen's use of SPECT brain scans.

Head Case: Why Has PBS Promoted Controversial Shrink
Dr. Daniel Amen? Observer, Richard Bernstein, 8/3/16. A
look into why PBS is such a fan of Dr. Daniel Amen and
his therapies.

Culver, Deanna. *Open Box Poetry.* CreateSpace (2018). A book of collective poems written by Deanna Culver designed to provide comfort or encouragement for those dealing with trauma.

Lipton, Bruce H., PhD. *The Biology of Belief: Unleashing the Power of Consciousness, Matter & Miracles.* Carlsbad, CA: Hay House, Inc. (2008). Lipton demonstrates how the new science of Epigenetics is shifting our understanding of how thoughts control life, thus offering a catalyst in how we think about our own thinking and how the brain's functioning and our cells are imprinted by our thoughts.

Josh M. Cisler, Keith Bush, G. Andrew James, Sonet Smitherman, Clinton D. Kilts. Decoding the Traumatic Memory among Women with PTSD: Implications for Neurocircuitry Models of PTSD and Real-Time fMRI Neurofeedback. PLOS ONE (August 4, 2015). PTSD is characterized by intrusive recall of the traumatic memory. This study has methodological implications for real-time fMRI neurofeedback of the trauma memory in PTSD and conceptual implications for neurocircuitry models of PTSD that attempt to explain core neural processing mechanisms mediating PTSD.

Sweeton, Jennifer. *Trauma Treatment Toolbox: 165 Brain-Changing Tips, Tools & Handouts to Move Therapy Forward.* Eau Claire, WI: PESI Publishing, 2019. Shows how to take a brain-based approach to trauma therapy, showing how to effectively heal the brain with straightforward, easy-to-implement treatment techniques. Each tool includes a short list of post trauma symptoms, relevant research, application, and tips on how to complete the exercise.

Visit the National Alliance on Mental Illness website to learn about all the different types of mental illnesses. As you read each description, you may feel like you have had all of the symptoms at one time or another. Keep in mind that these mental illnesses vary in intensity and severity. Think of them as being on a spectrum—there are severe and milder versions of each. Reviewing the different types of mental illnesses will be eye-opening for some and confirming for others. Always seek the advice of your physician or other qualified health provider with any questions you may have regarding a medical condition.

In-person therapy. As there is no one-size fits all type of therapy, check out the different options below. Each is unique in its offering.

Cognitive Behavioral Therapy

This type of therapy links your "automatic thoughts" to your feelings. The sessions are structured and focus on the problems (lack of sleep, anger, anxiety, difficulty at work, etc..) and the goals to set for the coming week. There is also a focus on the previous goals and the success that has been achieved. The relationship between therapist and client is more business oriented and equal, and is designed to be most effective with long-term problems and success.

Cognitive Processing Therapy

This therapy assists you in evaluating and changing the negative thoughts that stem from a trauma. By altering the way you think about your trauma, you change how you feel and are able to enjoy life.

Prolonged Exposure

This is a specific type of cognitive behavior therapy. The goal is to reduce traumatic experiences and reduce disturbances of severe PTSD and works well in cases where substance abuse is also present. Usually this is done in 90-minute weekly sessions over a 3-month period and includes reliving the trauma in a safe environment to separate the feelings and emotions associated with the trauma.

Eye Movement Desensitization and Reprocessing (EMDR)

This therapy works through reliving traumatic events in short, sequential doses while focusing on an outside stimulus or object, such as having your hand tapped and directed eye movement to desensitize the trauma.

Selective serotonin reuptake inhibitor

The goal of these medications for first-line therapy is to increase the amount of serotonin in the brain, thereby balancing mood, happiness and sense of well-being. Medications can help with depression, anxiety and sleep disorders. Four common medications are Zoloft, Paxil, Luvox and Prozac.

Watching/Listening:

What Parts of the Brain are Impacted by PTSD? (1:07) Michael Roy, MD, Col. (Ret.) explains how parts of the brain are affected by a traumatic experience.

What is Neuroplasticity? (3:14) It's possible to retrain your brain. This video explains what neuroplasticity is and why it's important.

First Responder with PTSD and the Value of a Brain Imaging Scan. (2:32) A first responder shares how a brain imaging scan helped him better understand what was going on in his brain and how the Amen Clinics created a treatment plan for him.

The Most Important Lesson from 83,000 Brain Scans, Daniel Amen, TEDx Talk. (14:36) In this popular TEDx Talk, Dr. Amen reveals what SPECT Brain Scans brings to the field of psychiatry and the benefits of seeing someone's brain scan prior to giving them a treatment plan.

SPECT Made Ridiculously Simple by Dr. Daniel Amen. (9:59) In this short video, psychiatrist Dr. Daniel Amen explains the origins of his work with brain SPECT imaging and how it changed psychiatry forever.

Conscious Content Collective. #Liftthestigma podcast series. (2:07) Brian Ross discusses the benefits of reminding yourself of the positive gains in life even in the midst of a dark time.

The Amen Clinics Method Described by Founder Dr. Daniel Amen. (12:48) This animated video describes how you can change your brain and subsequently your life.

Naked Podcaster with Kimberly Resch. (70 min.) Kimberly shares how Conscious Content came to be and shares a pretty significant trauma that happened at age 10.

Naked Podcaster with Brian Ross. (64 min.) Brian shares his motivation for Conscious Content and the traumas he's survived. Bottom line: he's like a cat who has lived nine lives.

Are You Disconnecting or Compartmentalizing? This blog looks and the pros and cons of compartmentalizing.

Stop the Stigma: A Conversation About Mental Health by CBS News. (33:49) In an effort to help break down stigmas surrounding mental health, "CBS This Morning" broadcasted a special live audience event. Guests include "Queer Eye" star Karamo Brown, a former social worker, mental health advocate and relationship expert who will discuss his experience with depression, and Cynthia Germanotta, who founded Born This Way Foundation with daughter Lady Gaga, about how mental illnesses affect a family.

Oprah Interviews Lady Gaga. (56:01) The two have an open, honest, and riveting conversation about mental health and self-care. This is part of Oprah's 2020 Vision Tour.

First Responder: PTSD Awareness. (9:28) Retired fireman and flight-medic first responder, Ray Norton, speaks candidly about the fire service and PTSD. The rapid increase in fire fighter suicide and the long term effects of trauma on a first responder have outnumbered retirement in this service field. Ray found a modality to help him offset stress and triggers, find out how.

Understanding PTSD's Effect on the Brain, Body, and Emotions. TEDx Talk by Dr. Janet Seahorn. (15:58). Dr. Seahorn shares the impact of PTSD on the brain, body, and emotions both from a researcher's point of view and as a spouse of a combat veteran.

Taking Action:

Visit www.amenclinics.com to learn more about Dr. Daniel Amen and SPECT brain scans as it helps determine a treatment plan.

To learn more about Dr. John King, his story, and his fight against PTSD including helpful videos and additional tools to combat PTSD.

Visit and get involved with your local chapter of the National Association of Mental Illness (NAMI) www. nami.org.

Look into getting an emotional support animal (ESA). If you have an emotional disability, you can legally qualify for an ESA. You must be certified as emotionally disabled by a psychologist, therapist, psychiatrist or other duly-licensed and/or certified mental health professional.

Subscribe to Tiffany Anderson's podcast and Facebook page The Phat Girl Chronicles where she bravely discusses life from a Phat Girl's POV.

Visit onemind.org. One Mind is a mental health non-profit that brings together the best minds in brain science and advocacy to accelerate brain research, and to create a world where all individuals facing brain health challenges can build healthy, productive lives.

Visit Born This Way Foundation. Cynthia Germanotta founded this nonprofit with daughter Lady Gaga about how mental illnesses affect a family. Speaks openly about dealing with PTSD and other mental illnesses.

Visit the American Psychological Association. This organization that is all about advancing psychology to benefit society and improve lives.

Free assessments to test anything from self-esteem, depression, ADHD, bipolar, etc. through PsychCentral or Psychology Today.

Online Therapy. If you've thought about seeking therapy before or tried it, but found it too expensive or not very effective, you might want to consider trying online therapy. There are many different options out there in many different price ranges. Some include Amwell, BetterHelp, Faithful Counseling, Regain, Talkspace, Pride Counseling, and Health Sapiens.

Learn about The Best PTSD Resources You Can Find Online. A resource for patients and families, Everyday Health helps by offering website options to use in conjunction with your doctor. Their goal is for people and their families suffering from PTSD to live healthy lives with happy relationships.

Visit PTSD Alliance, a website to find help wherever you are located. From a help desk, hotline, support groups, directories, and a mobile coaching app, they will help you get in touch with the right resources in your area.

PART IV

Hope: The Light

I know that each day is new, and our life works just like
nature. There are seasons. After the coldest, darkest winters,
springtime always comes and brings with it new
life and opportunity, a chance to live anew.

–Brian Ross

We do not receive wisdom, we must discover it for
ourselves, after a journey through the wilderness which
no one else can make for us, which no one can spare us,
for our wisdom is the point of view from which
we come at last to regard the world.

–Proust

The Oxford Dictionary describes hope as "a feeling of expectation and desire for a particular thing to happen." There is scientific proof that people who have hope do better in life, and it just may be the most important feeling state.

In previous chapters, we explored our lives being interrupted by circumstances beyond our control. We have introduced you to many different people who have shared their experience and knowledge, so you may be able to ask questions you didn't know to ask yourself before. This state of self-awareness is where all the magic is. When we're in this state of asking, the Universe must respond or present an answer. In short, if we ask the question, the answer is coming, so keep your heart open to the response.

I believe that hope with action is our catalyst to unlimited potential. This first step of self-awareness is where you'll begin to find your light in the darkness. Know that there will be setbacks, but you can create a better version of yourself by connecting the dots as they are presented to you. The goal is to remind yourself that power lies in your attitude of gratitude. We realize that hope is absolutely necessary for our healing journey.

Hope Wins Over Intelligence and Ability Alone

People often have a hard time wrapping their heads around the concept of hope. When we started to think about hope as a psychological vehicle to get us where we wanted to go, it started to make sense. After all, you could have the best engine ever in your car, but you won't get anywhere if you can't be bothered to drive it. Hope can get you to your desired destination. And it has certainly helped us along our journey.

Researchers who study positive psychology believe hope is the most important feeling state. Clinical psychologist Margaret Nagib, PsyD, says the following about hope:

Individuals who have significant levels of hope are more physically healthy and less susceptible to disease. They perform better academically and athletically. In fact, elite athletes score exceptionally high on psychological measures of hope, indicating that raw talent, grit, or even optimism without hope is insufficient when pursuing difficult goals. Research also indicates hope is positively correlated with self-esteem and healthier relationships. Hope increases the sense of meaning in life and identification and realization of goals and dreams even in the midst of adversity. Individuals with high hope set loftier goals and are more likely to realize them. That's because hope is a better predictor of success than intelligence or innate ability alone.[52]

With benefits like that, who wouldn't want to be hopeful?

The Science That Backs Up the Idea of Hope: Hope Theory

In 1991, Dr. C. R. Snyder, a psychology professor at the University of Kansas–Lawrence, came up with the Hope Theory which requires at least three components:

Focused thoughts

Strategies developed in advance to achieve these goals

The motivation to make the effort required to reach these goals

The more the person believes they can achieve the components listed above, the greater their chance of developing a feeling of hope. How hopeful are you? Dr. Snyder developed a Hope Test that takes about five minutes to complete. It measures your level of motivation and hope. See The Wisdom Well to access it.

Man never made any material as resilient
as the human spirit.

–Bernard Williams

Hope and the Human Spirit

We consider the human spirit to be a combination of hope, will, perseverance, and strength. The human spirit is resilient and can be put through trials and tribulations and persevere. Most often we find resiliency through connection to things like nature, community, our inner strengths, and something bigger than us like God or the Universe.

Kimberly Reflects on the Past Five Months

I feel the resilience of how change redirected my path to a place I never would have considered had this circumstance (of losing my son, Taylor) never happened. The Spirit is an incredible energy, so resilient and adaptable no matter the circumstances. As I reflect on my past, I recognize some of my conditioned behaviors such as loyalty, integrity, perseverance, and accountability have resulted from these one-off tragedies. Adversely, I have acquired panic attacks, a short temper, a lack of empathy for ignorance, and have been accused of holding people to impossible standards.

As I move forward, it is imperative that I continue to give myself grace and use Taylor's Spirit as an inspiration to keep moving forward. This path I have chosen isn't easy for me. It takes work to be so mindful, and many times I feel exhausted. The beauty of this entire situation is that gifts are coming daily from Taylor, and I am feeling honored to really see them.

Brian Shares His Perspective

What keeps me going? I have a strong belief in God, some reference it by other names, however, the God I believe in may be the same one you believe in. The God of Light and Love. The one who created the Universe and keeps our intricate bodies working without us thinking about it.

I know that each day is new, and our life works just like nature. There are seasons. After the coldest, darkest winters, springtime always comes and brings with it new life and opportunity, a chance to live anew.

There is something amazing and awe inspiring about the human spirit. No matter what we seem to deal with in life, if we are able to find hope and purpose and have faith in something bigger than ourselves, we as humans can find the energy and drive to move forward even if we are required to completely recreate ourselves with all new surroundings and a new set of rules. I see it every day with people, and I believe it will be required in this new reality we are finding ourselves in.

I know that it's possible to get through tough situations, whether they be the loss of loved ones, divorce, the loss of successful businesses that lead to losing my mind and the basic ability to provide food and shelter for a short time. It requires believing in something larger than yourself that you can create a purpose around.

For me, it's always been my faith in God, my love for my kids, and now it also includes my love and respect for my best friend, Kimberly. I have found that the stories in your head that tell you that it's not possible to fade away if you lean forward into life, instead, your new reality will begin to take shape. In some cases, this new reality is far bigger and better than you could have imagined.

Brian Affirms the Value of Mindfulness

Earlier, I shared stories about my life almost being cut short. Life can be beautiful and profound; however, it can become serious when you least expect it. When you do experience something difficult, it helps to be mindful and grounded in the moment.

There is a lot of research to support that there is no reason to panic when confronted with something new or out of the ordinary. Things generally aren't as bad as our brain can make them seem. Have you ever wondered why we sometimes overreact to a situation? Our brains tend to create worse-case scenarios when we most likely still have options if we're able to think clearly.

The fight, flight, or freeze response happens when our brain perceives a threat and goes into protection mode. Our ancestors from long ago may have had to run from a lion or a bear to survive. This built-in survival response pumps the body with adrenaline and other chemicals, temporarily giving us the strength and endurance to run fast, put up our dukes, or stay perfectly still. Nowadays, our fear or stressor usually isn't a bear but something more mundane, like a deadline or sitting in heavy traffic when we need to be in a meeting. But our bodies still respond as if we need to run.

We think much more rationally when we are calm and not in fight-or-flight mode. Being mindful is one way to recognize whether we're dealing with a bear or running late for a meeting. It can instantly bring us to a state of calm.

It's also been my experience that having faith that God has my back in difficult situations helps me stay planted in the moment so I can see my options with a clear mind and execute on them when necessary.

Ray of Light

When you're feeling anxious and don't feel grounded. Bring yourself back to the present moment by practicing the following exercise:

Sit down at your desk or a table.
Hold out your hands and look at all of your fingers and wiggle them.
Now place them down on the desk or table.
How does the surface feel on the palms of your hand?
Is it cold or warm?
Is it smooth or rough?
Now notice the color of the surface.
Is the space you're in cool or is it warm?

Close your eyes and inhale, envisioning the incoming breath as light and exhale out what no longer serves you. Notice how the air feels entering your nose and the release of the air from your mouth. Repeat this as many times as necessary to feel calm and grounded back into the present moment.

Fishing in The Wisdom Well

To determine whether somebody is an optimist or pessimist, some psychologists conduct a simple test with a glass of water. Optimists typically say the glass is half-full, and pessimists usually say it's half-empty. Optimists tend to focus on the positive: There is still water available to drink!

One night I dreamed I was walking along the beach with the Lord. Many scenes from my life flashed across the sky. In each scene I noticed footprints in the sand. Sometimes there were two sets of footprints, other times there was one only.
This bothered me because I noticed that during the low periods of my life, when I was suffering from anguish, sorrow or defeat, I could see only one set of footprints, so I said to the Lord, "You promised me Lord, that if I followed you, you would walk with me always. But I have noticed that during the most trying periods of my life there has only been one set of footprints in the sand. Why, when I needed you most, have you not been there for me?"
The Lord replied, "The years when you have seen only one set of footprints, my child, is when I carried you.

–Mary Stevenson, 1936

What's God Got to Do with It?

When our world is falling apart, it's comforting to know that there's something much bigger than us who can help share the burden. For some, that's God, Buddha, Allah, Nature, or the Universe.

Some people refer to themselves as spiritual while others refer to themselves as religious. What's the difference between the two? Religious people worship God or some kind of deity and have a personal set of religious attitudes, beliefs, and practices. Spirituality involves a connection to something larger than you and believing you are in charge of your destiny. Spiritual people often look to nature connection.

Research shows that religion and spirituality are good for your health. Dr. Harold Koenig of Duke University contends that as people pray and ask God for guidance, they feel a sense of control over their situation, helping them cope with depression and anxiety.[53]

Researchers at the Mayo Clinic concluded, "Most studies have shown that religious involvement and spirituality are associated with better health outcomes, including greater longevity, coping skills, and health-related quality of life (even during terminal illness) as well as less anxiety, depression, and suicide. Several studies have shown that addressing the spiritual needs of the patient may enhance recovery from illness."[54]

> I think belief and faith are very, very important. I think we undervalue the spiritual aspects of us as human beings.
>
> –Dr. John A. King

Each of Us Has a Different Faith Journey

Dr. Carol Drake Wheatley knows a thing or two about faith: she established Power in the Workplace Ministries, a non-profit corporation in Florida, over twenty-five years ago. Power in the Workplace is an affiliated ministry through the American Evangelistic Association, the Billy Graham Rapid Response Team, and the Association of Related Ministries Inc. Not only is she an ordained minister, crisis response chaplain, and an ordained senior chaplain, she is certified in both individual and group crisis intervention. She is also a certified business mentor through the U.S. Small Business Administration.

We wanted to learn more about how faith can help us heal. Dr. Wheatley is a friend of ours, so we sat down with her to talk about the power of faith and how it helps create hope. Spoiler alert: There's a door-to-door vacuum cleaner salesman involved.

Dr. Wheatley's Faith Journey Story, In Her Words

Faith wasn't always something that I took for granted. I grew up in a middle-class neighborhood living a block from the beach. My childhood was a great one. I went on to marry and had three children and had what I considered a good life, but I always knew there was something desperately missing.

One by one, God began to send people into my life. The first person was a vacuum cleaner salesman. Really . . . a vacuum cleaner salesman knocked on my door. He started talking about Jesus and asked, "Have you made Jesus the Lord of your life?" I looked him square in the eye and said "yes," even though I was lying through my teeth. It became a self-fulfilling prophecy. After that, it was one person after another who came to me and planted the seed of God. I asked myself repeatedly, *I wonder if this could be God talking to me?*

Finally, one day, my friend said, "Why don't you just come to church with me?" I just kind of rolled my eyes and said, "Yeah, whatever." I went and that's when I realized that I hadn't gone to church, instead I'd gone home. I was where I belonged. It was overwhelming. That was over forty years ago. It filled my heart and I found incredible strength. I always saw myself as a kind of a wallflower and weak person. I soon realized I'm not. I'm this powerhouse. Once

I learned that God had filled me with His power and given me the authority to use it, everything in my life changed.

Just because you've made the decision to be a child of God doesn't mean that everything magically gets okay and there are no issues or troubles in your life. That's just unrealistic because stuff happens. That was the case with me, too, as my husband and I divorced several years later.

Does hope translate in faith? First, we have to understand there is hope, but there is something beyond "just" hope, and that's the realization of the things that we hope for. Faith is simply another way of saying, "Okay, God, I trust you." That's what faith is. Faith is the substance of things hoped for, and the evidence of the things that we can't see yet.

When we talk about hope, that is the end result. Faith is what creates it. So, faith and hope go hand in hand. I host a Bible study in my home called, "Interested in God? Not So Interested in Church?" I invite people to come and get their questions answered and be a part of fellowship. I do encourage people to go to church because the Bible tells us that we need each other, but you can't learn in an hour a week all there is to know about God. For your experience to be powerful, you need to understand how to live in the kingdom of God.

Simply listening to someone talk about God won't necessarily give us the hope we need. It takes a change of heart and a change in how we think. Hope comes when we have faith in God and faith comes by hearing His word.

Chaplains use the term Ministry of Presence. Essentially, it's just being there for someone. One of my chaplain friends called me several months after a twenty-nine-year-old security guard killed forty-nine people and wounded fifty-three others in a mass shooting on June 12, 2016, inside Pulse, a gay nightclub in Orlando, Florida. He and I had both been there to comfort family, loved ones, and the wounded. He asked me if he could come by and talk to me.

After a two-hour drive, he got to my home and he just sat there without saying anything. I didn't say anything either. I was just there for him until he was ready to download. Once he was ready, it all came out.

Sometimes we have to know enough not to say a thing. If you have a rotten day, sometimes you just need someone to sit there with you.

The most important thing that moves the heart of God is our faith. Have faith in God. Change the way you think by reading the Bible. Forgive those you need to forgive. Be grateful for what you have. Do these things and God will change your life.

Hope is being able to see that there is
light despite all of the darkness.

–Desmond Tutu, cleric and human rights activist

Kimberly's Journey into the Light

From a young age of two or three, I can remember being visited by Spirits or energies others couldn't see. At first they scared me, but as time passed, I became pretty familiar with them being around. It was like never being alone. We seemed to have an understanding of occupying space together without interruption. I was thinking they were the Holy Ghost. I allowed pretty much every exchange without question or understanding at the time.

As a young teenager, I was more unsettled with the energies in my space and sometimes would feel agitated, and their energy seemed to mirror mine. I was attracting the energy I was transmitting. I began to question this gift I had. It was no longer a warm fuzzy exchange but a demanding, relentless one. I could no longer share space in harmony. I felt watched and crowded. Sometimes, feelings of paranoia came to me. I was unsure how to handle the change in my relationship to this energy.

It wasn't until I was much older that I understood that what I was witnessing were Souls needing to pass through the "veil" to go where they needed to. Wherever that was, I knew I couldn't judge or get to decide. The information was simply moving through me. I was a conduit.

This dense energy matter was left after the body was exhausted and laid to rest, it felt like I was a stop on their spiritual train heading somewhere. Most of these energies seem to have passed over suddenly—or experienced an immediate exchange from body to spirit after having been in an accident or for some other reason. They lacked a transition period from this frequency to whatever the next stop was for them.

Some days were busier than others. I was still never alone. Did I mention I had a full-time job, kids, a husband, and a house to take care of?

Questions started to come up within myself as I observed the unsettled nature of this matter in my space. It was changing as I was changing. My observations were becoming more acute and I started "seeing" more. It wasn't until I was twenty-nine that I started to put the pieces together or even really talk about it. I do remember my mom talking about having experiences like this, but I never really asked her about them.

I thought I might be going crazy. Out of desperation, I went to a psychic and he observed me and told me I wasn't alone. My response was something like," No kidding!" I then asked him a very direct question, "What do they want and why do they find me?"

His response was, "They think you're the light."

My response to this was, "Yeah, okay, great. Now what?"

He was very clear with his recommendation. "Ask them what they need, if they have any messages to share, and if they were ready to go to the light." Still not buying in, I got up and told him that was enough information for me now and that I had enough responsibility already. I paid him and his final words of advice were, "Just try it. Everyone benefits. I promise, you can do this. Just trust the process. You'll know what to do."

One minute later, I got into my car and felt as if I were in one of those cars stuffed with clowns. I was literally buried under energy to the point where I couldn't drive. So I sucked it up, put the car back in park, and asked the energy hitchhikers these questions: "What did they need? Did they have any messages to share? Were they ready to go to the light?" It was literally a sound off with everyone talking over each other in my head. I was still in the parking lot.

Feeling overwhelmed, I yelled in an embarrassingly loud voice: "Everyone get out of my car and get into the imaginary bus. The Angels will greet you and take you to your correct astral plane. Do not stop, just keep it moving. I send you to the light and validate you. Go in peace."

Then everything stopped. It was like a vacuum of silence for the first time in my entire life.

I was reeling from the words that came out of my mouth. I wasn't sure where they came from except it wasn't from thinking. From that moment, I felt I needed a strong relationship with God, an energy source to help me with this newfound job. So I enrolled in seminary and learned whatever I could as a backup in case I ever needed an arsenal of Angels from Heaven. At this point, I was confirming that anything was possible.

Answers unfolded, as life will if you're open to it. Daily, I would have occurrences and started creating systems and procedures to events I was encountering. I asked endless questions to the ether—whenever something came to mind—and received answers that had to be written down using words and phrases I never used before.

I remember thinking that I might be crazy, but I was feeling purpose and drive to dig deeper and learn what was beyond my five senses. The more I asked, the more I learned. I never read a book to compare my experience with others' out of fear I would be jaded by someone else's opinion. I now know that many books support the process I used, and I had no idea.

Years went by and my skill set expanded exponentially. I created a consulting service to read energy and send people to their proper place that had passed called Angels Influence. That responsibility has taken me around the world to help really beautiful people who needed the kind of guidance you can't get from a traditional doctor's office. I did that for several years and sometimes still do. I have shared experiences and skills along the way with people as the situations present themselves. My younger two kids grew up with me doing this, and they didn't know any different.

Taylor, since he was my youngest, had the most exposure to me working with these Souls. He understood it was an honor to help them pass. He confirmed he never saw any of them, but he accepted it as something I did to help. It was no surprise that when he died, he waited until I was ready to see him. Nearly three weeks had passed, and now he needed help with his lesson and to be guided to his next destination.

It was the hardest thing I think God could have asked me for, with some pondering of "what is the heartbreaking lesson" for me doing this? In my clearest state, I realized he was reminding me that we are evolutionary and in honoring the process I was gifted, I was receiving. I was able to assist with this most important exchange.

My faith in God and the intricacies of the human spirit have blessed me in ways I could never express except with gratitude. It's a completely different way to look at life and death—not as finite as we have been taught for generations but as transitional. Witnessing Taylor's transition after all the trauma I had been feeling the previous twenty-one days was a massive blessing for me. It may have been the only way I could let his energy go. The energetic cords that bound us together as mother and son were strong. It was a blessing as it was a clean transition and so humbling to witness.

If you are feeling pressure and a mood change happens perhaps you are the light an energy sees and you too can help it transition. First, ask yourself if you feel alone. Say this prayer, "I call Energies 600 or higher on the scale of consciousness to be with me at this time, to fill me with light. I clear any and all energies that no longer serve me and send them to the correct astral plane in which they deserve. By the power of my free will and by the power of God I release you, go in peace. Amen."

By saying this prayer that I simply made up over time and experience, I began to feel immediately lighter. Some days I didn't feel a change at all. Some days I said the prayer one hundred times to get through the day. It's really a personal experience. However, as I was developing it, I was realizing that the mood swings that I was having were going away when I did this prayer on a regular basis. I felt clean and calm.

The Serenity Prayer helps me too. I'm just in the process of accepting things I cannot change, knowing the things I can and asking for wisdom to know the difference.

My faith in God and the process of life and death with this body are infinite. Anything is possible when we have this body, and anything is possible when we leave it. The hope is that we are never gone but are transformed into light. And that light blesses us each day in the sunrise, the loon in the lake you see on your morning ride, or the eagle that flies overhead when you least expect it. They are all reminders. I am sure you have noticed your own reminders. Allow them to help you find peace in the moment.

Ray of Light

Tips for difficult or significant days.

"I'm _____ , and I'm _____ years old. I'm in a safe place in (town), (state) . I'm with _____, and he/she/they care for me. There's no one in my life who wants to hurt me. I can cry and be scared, and everyone will still love and accept me. I need to have these feelings so I can let them go. I may feel them repeatedly, but each time I need to accept them so I can let them go. If I am feeling guilt, shame, or other painful feelings, I don't have to believe that I am guilty or did something shameful or whatever. I can say to myself, "Isn't that sad. I am feeling an old pattern I grew up with, but I need to feel it, so it will pass."

—Patience Mason

Sacred Nourishment: Turning from Hopeless to Hopeful

As humans, we all experience moments of hopelessness. That's normal. Holistic nutritionist Annah Pelot shares how hope to restore wholeness is within reach if we are open to it.

Annah Pelot

No matter how out of order we have become from trauma or negative experiences, the reset to order is available from vibrations within the natural forces around us. We are in a constant state of vibrational connection with all things. Some connections have order and structure; others are chaotic and disorganized. As awareness grows, we begin to recognize and make associations to what supports order and what does not.

In ancient communities such as the Nasarean Essenes (Nasarean=to lift up and Essene=healing way), their daily mindful practices connected them to vibrational patterns of order. Generation upon generation living in communion with the natural laws gave rise to physical, mental, and emotional health and expanded spiritual conscious growth. We too have all the tools they did.

They organized these elements into what is called the Tree of Life where there are seven branches and seven roots, each representing an element of natural order. Each day of the week and each morning and evening they purposefully connected with a cosmic and earth element. This practice created a conscious rhythm that allowed them to live long, healthy balanced lives.[56]

Ray of Light

A daily practice of going outside and watching the sunrise can be powerful for transforming the weight of depression. The morning sunrise awakens energy from the base of the spine to the crown of the head. Try slowly moving your hands up your body as the sun is rising and end with them over your head. Imagine the rays of the sun awakening every cell of your being with vibrant life energy. Three minutes of mindfully being present at the sunrise of each morning uplifts the whole day. Receiving the solar rays within our bodies with intention to use this power to direct our actions in support of the highest good is life changing. Expect to experience an increase in inspired purposeful action.

Light is a really strong metaphor for hope, and every human being deserves that sense of hope, that sense of light in their life. We do not receive wisdom. We gain wisdom after a journey that no one else can take for us or with us. That becomes honoring every other person's story. Sometimes when you're in the darkness, it's important that you address it. Yes, you're in the darkness, but don't stay there. Don't build your house there. There's always hope.

–Janet Seahorn

It's time to take a sip from The Wisdom Well.

Note all the resources listed here can be accessed on https://Consciouscontent.org by clicking on the Wisdom Well Resources link.

THE WISDOM WELL

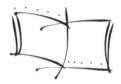

Reading:

NICABM Free Resources. NICABM Free Resources.Blog posts and other free resources to learn more about how to treat trauma and the symptoms that accompany it.

Snyder, C.R. *Psychology of Hope: You Can Get There from Here*, NY: The Free Press, 1994. In the *Psychology of Hope*, a professor of psychology reveals the specific character traits that produce highly hopeful individuals. He offers a test to measure one's level of optimism and gives specific advice on how to become a more hopeful person.

Hope: How to Find It Huffpost.com blog post. Trust that there is hope and learn how to create momentum and mental positivity which can only lead to a better future.

Strauss, Jennifer and Lang, Ariel. Complementary and Alternative Treatments for PTSD. PTSD Research

Quarterly: 23(2), 2012. This article goes in depth about complementary and alternative treatments (CAM) such as acupuncture, meditation, and relaxation as well as how they interact with traditional therapies.

Baer, Drake. The Father of Mindfulness on What Mindfulness Has Become. An Interview with Jon Kabat-Zinn, creator of Mindfulness Based Stress Reduction. (6-minute read) Blog on Medium.com.

How Virtual Reality Exposure Treats PTSD. Virtual Reality Exposure Therapy (VRET) is used to target behaviors and their triggers by confronting fears and phobias that cause anxiety. Utilizing computer generated programs creates a safe space to experience these situations.

How to Treat PTSD Naturally. Acupuncture Massage College. Nov. 6, 2016. (blogpost). The article refers to different natural options including acupuncture, Reiki, Tai chi, biofeedback, hypnosis, guided imagery, and relaxation therapy.

Benarous, Isabelle. *Break the Code of Your Illness.* Bioreprogramming Press, 2019. The author offers a synthesis of major breakthroughs regarding the origin of health disorders. Illness can now be understood through a new paradigm that can permit individuals to directly take control of their health through self-awareness and perceptual changes. The author's research uncovers the undeniable logic of an unprecedented approach regarding the mind-body connection and reveals new hypotheses regarding ancestral impacts as well as in-utero distress and the type of effects they can produce in one's life.

Wheatley, Carol. *Why Churches Die…and How to Resurrect Them: Stop Blaming the Millennials for Everything!* Power in the Workplace Ministries, Inc., 2019.

Wheatley, Carol. Twisted Roots, *Twisted Lives: How the Delusion of Demonic Power Defeats Us.* Power in the Workplace Ministries, Inc., 2019. Are you frustrated after running into the same problem in your life over and over again? Are there certain patterns in your life that you want to change? This book looks at how we might open ourselves up to demonic influences, why this happens, and best of all, how to get rid of it.

Koenig, Harold. *The Healing Power of Faith: How Belief and Prayer Can Help You Triumph Over Disease.* NY: Touchstone, 1999. An infirm, lifetime alcoholic suddenly becomes sober and strong. A patient undergoing open-heart surgery amazes the doctors with a speedy convalescence. A cancer patient given only a few months to live defies the predictions. What accounts for such remarkable recoveries? Is it a miracle or medicine? Dr. Harold G. Koenig presents groundbreaking scientific evidence that provides answers to these puzzling medical mysteries.

Hay, Louise L. *Heal Your Body: the Mental Causes for Physical Illness and the Metaphysical Way to Overcome Them.* Carlsbad, CA: Hay House, 2012. This reference book assists people in linking physical ailments to core mental unresolved stress, and suggests new thought patterns in the form of positive affirmations. The correlating body-mind affirmations are powerful and supportive in reinforcing new life-giving thoughts.

Newton, Michael, Ph.D. *Journey of Souls: Case Studies of Life between Lives.* Woodbury, MN: Llewellyn Publications. 2012. Dr. Newton is a seasoned hypnotherapist. As he worked with thousands of PTSD subjects to reach their hidden memories, they went to the hereafter. Those under deep hypnotherapy describe what happens after death. This remarkable book is based on like case studies of thousands of subjects and chronicles the journey of the soul, chapter by chapter. It has assisted many grieving transitioned loved ones come to a place of deeper peace.

Pert, Candace B., Ph.D. *Molecules of Emotion: The Science behind Mind-Body Medicine.* NY: Scribner. (1997). This book offers grounding support in identifying why we feel the way we feel and how our thoughts and emotions affect our well-being. Pert's pioneering research propels decisive answers to these questions and demonstrates how chemicals inside our cells form an information network linking our thoughts, body and mind. Her work establishes a biomolecular basis for our emotions and a rational for healing modalities that lie outside of traditional models.

Pfeiffer, Carl C. *Nutrition and Mental Illness: An Orthomolecular Approach to Balancing Body Chemistry.* Rochester, Vermont: Healing Arts Press, 1988. Believing that drugs and psychoanalysis were not always the best course of treatment for a variety of mental illnesses, Dr. Carl Pfeiffer began an extensive program of research into the causes and treatment of mental illness, and opened the Brain Bio Center in Princeton, New Jersey. Here, with a team of scientists, he found that many psychological problems can be traced to biochemical imbalances in the body. This book documents his approach.

Watching/Listening:

Science Says: Religion May Be Good For Your Health. (6:06) Mayo Clinic shares research that religion and spirituality is good for your health.

Hope Theory: Make Your Life Better. (3:44) Successful goal setting using hope theory.

The Theta Code. Filled with amazing stories of healing and regeneration, along with practical step-by-step exercises to unlock your theta code, this program will be your guide to healing and wellness in areas you never thought possible. You'll move out of stress, illness, and disease and easily step into improved health, greater vitality, and renewed joy in your life!

The Wisdom of Trauma. (3:21) This movie trailer for a transformative documentary features Dr. Gabor Mate where he exposes what is really going on underneath our trauma. He makes a plea for trauma informed medicine and education in this world.

Hope Floats (Trailer). (2:18) A 1998 movie where Birdee Pruitt (Sandra Bullock) has been humiliated on live television by her best friend, Connie (Rosanna Arquette), who's been sleeping with Birdee's husband, Bill (Michael Paré). Birdee tries starting over with her daughter, Bernice (Mae Whitman), by returning to her small Texas hometown, but she's faced with petty old acquaintances who are thrilled to see Birdee unhappy — except for her friend Justin (Harry Connick Jr.). As he helps Birdee get back on her feet, love begins to blossom.

Oprah SuperSoul Conversations. Hear Oprah's personal selection of her interviews with thought-leaders, best-selling authors, spiritual luminaries, as well as health and wellness experts. All designed to light you up, guide you through life's big questions and help bring you one step closer to your best self.

Taking Action:

Measure how much hope you have in this simple 5-minute test using Dr. Snyder's Hope Theory.

Take a short quiz to measure how hopeful you are. The quiz How Hopeful Are You? was created by Stacy Kaiser, a successful Southern California-based licensed psychotherapist, author, relationship expert, and media personality.

Trauma-informed yoga. Locate a yoga instructor who has been trained by Warriors at Ease to provide trauma-informed yoga. Plug your zip code and address in and you'll be instantly connected with someone near you. If there isn't someone near you, simply Google trauma-informed yoga instructors in your area.

Visit Dr. Kari Uselman's Wellness Essentials business. Her mission is to positively support those seeking holistic wellness become empowered in their life journeys so they may live fully with purpose and joy.

Check out Naturopathic Doctors through the American Association of Naturopathic Physicians. Naturopathic doctors are educated and trained in accredited naturopathic medical colleges. They diagnose, prevent, and treat acute and chronic illness to restore and establish optimal health by supporting the person's inherent self-healing process. Rather than just suppressing symptoms, naturopathic doctors work to identify underlying causes of illness, and develop personalized treatment plans to address them.

Visit Twisted Sage. They manufacture consciousness tools such as a 5G Energetic Transformation Kit. You can shop for products on their website.

PART V

Support: The Lift

The greatest good you can do for another is not just
share your riches, but reveal to them their own.

-Author unknown

So far, we've covered how carrying trauma through our lives can have devastating consequences on our body, mind, and spirit. In this part of the book, we will provide integrative healing practices you can do at home. The goal is to find what resonates with you and try it out. Recovery from trauma doesn't have to be a dark road. You can learn, share your journey with others, and even have fun while getting healthy.

This chapter shares alternative healing therapies and techniques, along with more stories, that weave together mind, body, and spirit. They (mind, body, spirit) are integral, not separate from each other, and when one aspect of our Being becomes distressed, it imprints upon the whole.

Trauma is devastating to the human spirit, but the human spirit is strong and has an innate drive for meaningful purpose. You matter. Your story matters. Your Light and your gifts matter. We believe in you. In this chapter, you'll learn nurturing and nourishing techniques that promote much-needed healing. Blessings to you on your journey to wholeness as you navigate the path home to yourself.

Thinking Outside the Box: Exploring Alternative Therapies for PTSD

Integrative medicine combines different treatment approaches such as traditional Western and Eastern medicine practices, as well as newer alternative approaches.

Integrative medicine looks at the individual treatment needs of each patient. As the results are promising, we wanted to share with you a more thorough exploration of integrated approaches to trauma treatment. We begin with a technique called SomatoEmotional Release.

SomatoEmotional Release to Free Trauma Stored in Body Memory

As someone who is nationally certified in Biofeedback and Complex Homeopathy, Kari Uselman weaves together her knowledge, intuition, and skills to meet her client's needs. What we like about Kari is her thirst for knowledge and helping people. She has personally helped us both.

We spoke during the pandemic of 2020, and she shared her concern for people not being fully aware of the trauma that the pandemic was bringing and how it could bring on PTSD. She is a firm believer that our bodies have a lot of answers if we just listen to them. She also sees a link between emotional distress and generational health problems.

When first meeting with clients, Kari does an extensive intake process to learn as much about her client as possible. She asks a lot of questions and listens intently to the responses. Working in this field has been life changing for Kari. She continues to educate herself on the newest tools to help inspire people to live consciously and make a positive difference through holistic wellness support, advocacy, and education. Her passion is assisting others transform stress into fuel for wellbeing.

Kari has a vast holistic toolbox that includes FDA-approved quantum science devices and SomatoEmotional Release techniques that support stress reduction and a return to balance emotionally, physically, mentally, and spiritually.

She shared a case study with us where she used her analytic and intuitive skills to help free a forty-year-old man from debilitating back pain. When she first met with the man, he was looking at back surgery. Physical therapy and acupuncture were not helping, and his pain was so intense that he was not able to work his plumbing job or drive his race car. He was trying to avoid surgery at all costs and so called on Kari.

In Her Own Words: Kari Explains What Happened in a Session

As I began his session with quantum biofeedback, drowning presented in the top ten stress reactions in a comprehensive holistic list of over 15,000. I asked him if somebody close to him drowned or if he ever had a near drowning experience. He responded "no." That's when I went onto another technique called craniosacral therapy, weaving in SomatoEmotional Release.

SomatoEmotional Release assists the tissue and cells to release stored memories and holding patterns of protection when the brain is unable to process a solution. This technique is one of many modalities that offers a solution to core traumas, which draws upon foundations of biological decoding.

As I assessed his body and held my hands on his lumbar spine, I noticed stillness. There was no movement in his cerebral spinal fluid. When this happens, it is a profound opportunity for release, remediation, and healing. I asked, "What are you thinking about?" He responded that he was being pulled up by a riptide. When I asked him how old he was, he responded twenty-three. I kept asking questions.

He was on spring break with his buddies, and he got pulled up on the riptide and he thought he was going to die. Somehow, he didn't. But, that fear of dying lodged into his spine. My client had just turned forty, and he always thought he would die at the age of forty, which was a feeling unrelatable to any physical ailment, yet it triggered the subconscious memory of his experience at age twenty-three, which manifested the stored "pain" in his spine.

As we talked, it was as if his cells were saying, "Okay, that was seventeen years ago. You're safe now. Thank you so much, tissue and cells, for keeping me safe, but I don't need the protection pattern anymore." And at that moment the pain left his body. He got off the table with no pain and the pain never returned.

This technique has assisted trauma release in many of my clients over the years, and it is always amazing to witness the transformation.[57]

Equine Therapy

We met with Scott Bill, President of the Brian Bill Foundation, who is a proponent for using equine therapy to help people with PTSD combat veterans.

Scott Bill, President of the Brian Bill Foundation, Shares How Horses Can Help with PTSD

My grandfather raised horses. I had my first horse, a pony, when I was five years old. I grew up on horses, and I have a love for horses and what they teach [people] and the relationship between them. Equine therapy became the nucleus of our program. My son Brian, after ten years in the SEAL teams, was getting post-traumatic stress disorder. As I traveled, I found more and more guys had combat PTSD, regular PTSD, and I thought my time would be better served getting these guys together and helping them deal with the issues that they have.

Horses are very tender and emotional, on alert all the time. We teach them how to address the horse, and tell them to not be afraid of the horse, because they can tell that in a second. Just be open and friendly to the horse, and they will reciprocate. That's their trigger. They will feel, "Oh, the trigger's okay. I can talk to him," or, "I can stand there."

We're teaching how to put the bridle on, how to put the saddle on, how to clean the horse's hooves, how to make the horse comfortable with you. At the same time, by you doing these things, you get comfortable with the horse. Your triggers, like, "Oh, he's so big. He's going to push me and jump me and kick me"—your triggers will go away too. You realize, "He's not going to do that to me, he trusts me and we have a relationship."

When you get on that horse for the first time and you're shaking a little bit, but the horse knows and trusts you, and then you walk off with the horse, and you're brothers, here together. It's a wonderful thing.[58]

Accelerated Resolution Therapy

Another successful modality is Accelerated Resolution Therapy (ART). ART reprograms how the brain stores traumatic memories. The treatment uses eye movements to help bring new information into existing memories.

Nutrition and Brain Health

We know that eating nutritious foods helps us stay physically healthy. Many researchers have linked food to brain health as well. We talked to some of our experts to help fill us in on how diet can help with PTSD.

Heal the Gut, Heal the Brain

Kari Uselman shared something that isn't often discussed in the world of Western medicine—the gut-brain connection. With a proper diet that avoids consuming pesticides and genetically modified organisms (GMOs), and introduces certain nutrients and microbes, we can heal the gut and protect the brain from mental imbalances. We sat down with her to learn more.

In Her Own Words: Kari Uselman, PhD

The quality of our food has shifted over the past several decades with the introduction of a widely used herbicide in the United States, Roundup [glyphosate], and GMOs, which are plants, animals, or microorganisms whose genetic material has been altered in a way that does not occur naturally. I started to pay closer attention when one of my clients told me she was allergic to apples. I challenged her to experiment with organic apples to discern a similar reaction. There was none, to her delight.

Most conventional apples (and other fruits and vegetables) are laden with pesticides and/or a variety of wax coatings, neither of which are life-giving to the human body. Animals and birds stay away from GMO crops. Did you know that glyphosate explodes the digestive tracts of insects and is correlated to leaky gut in humans?

When the body does not digest and assimilate the nutrients from food, amino acids do not make it to the brain to be converted into neurotransmitters, which feed brain neural pathways. Lack of neurotransmitters in the brain correlate to malaise, depression, and other mental imbalances. Clean, organic non-GMO food can return the brain and gut to balance.

My favorite nutritional supports to remediate leaky gut are fulvic and humic acid and AFA blue green algae, which is one of the most nutrient and protein dense foods on the planet.

There are many research-based references to substantiate my observations and suggestions for gut remediation. The biggest gut brain wreckers are GMO wheat, soy, and oils. When the gut is healthy, the brain is sustained, stress is more manageable, healing is supported, and life flows with more ease, grace, and harmony.[59]

You Are What You Eat

Annah Pelot, a holistic nutritionist with a bachelor of science in community and medical dietetics, is an advocate of life-giving nutrition and practices. The work of holistic lifestyle advocates Edmond Bordeaux Szekely and Gabriel Cousens, MD, inspired her to view food from a whole new perspective.

We met with Annah, who believes that food is more than just fuel for our body. It is a tool for conscious growth as it contributes to our physical, emotional, mental, and spiritual health. She shared how non-GMO seeds, grains, nuts, and beans, when soaked and sprouted, convert inorganic minerals into life-giving substances our bodies can use. Below, we provide examples of each:

Seeds: sunflower, sesame, pumpkin, alfalfa, mung, broccoli, radish, clover, quinoa, chia, flaxseed

Grains: wheat, rye, rice, oats, millet, barley

Raw Nuts: almonds, walnuts, pecans, cashews, pine nuts, brazil nuts

Beans and peas: black, pinto, garbanzo, and navy beans; lentils; dried and black-eyed peas

These foods also supply carbohydrates, protein, fats, enzymes, vitamins, and hormones in a form the body can assimilate. The life essence of these foods is like a new-born child. They are energetically abundant! For sprouting guidelines check out this link, www.sproutpeople.org.

There are life-sustaining foods, life-slowing foods (cooked), and life-diminishing foods. For your best health and healing, it's good to know the difference.[60]

Life-Sustaining Foods

These are fresh fruits, vegetables and greens, which are rich in minerals, vitamins, enzymes, carbohydrates, protein, fat, and water. These foods are like a wise adult with the elements that hold our energy stable. These include:

Fruits: apples, pears, peaches, apricots, plums, oranges, lemons, limes, grapefruits, mangos, papayas, pineapples, strawberry raspberries, currants, blackberries, blueberries, grapes, watermelons, cantaloupes, honeydews, dates, figs, olives, tomatoes, cucumbers, peppers

Vegetables: carrots, cabbages, beets, kohlrabi, cauliflower, broccoli, celery, greens, herbs, potatoes, sweet potatoes

For creative ways to use fresh fruits and vegetables, check out The Wisdom Well at the end of this chapter.

Life-Slowing Foods (Cooked)

Cooking food brings comfort and warmth and enhances flavor. However, vital nutrients such as vitamins and enzymes are lost by high heat and prolonged cooking, especially frying. To preserve vital nutrients and enjoy the warmth of cooked food, lightly steam or cook at a low temperature of 130 degrees or less. For healthy recipes, visit The Wisdom Well.

Life-Diminishing Foods

Processed white sugar, white flour, foods sprayed with chemicals in the growing process, artificial colors, flavors, preservatives, GMOs, and animal products can lead to leaky gut as well as affect the body's capacity to maintain physical and mental vitality. Check out The Wisdom Well. to find 100 life-diminishing foods.

The Philosophy Behind Conscious Food Choices: In Annah's Words

May the feeling of hope be with you as you journey down the path of conscious food choices. Be kind to yourself as you ebb and flow each day. Call on your will to be strengthened as you begin to see what it takes to become your brightest Self. Start the day with a vibrant, nourishing self-care recipe. You are worthy!

Every living plant carries a vibrational message. As we eat these living foods, we are receiving messages of order and structure that keep us vibrating in harmony with the natural environment. This pathway advocates a plant-based lifestyle. Animals are seen as our younger brothers and sisters on the journey of evolution. Humanity is called to live in harmony with them, not harm them. This became a reality for me when I educated myself on the current system of mass production of animals. Studies of the meat showed high levels of adrenaline hormone in the animal's flesh as they experience fear and the fight or flight response before processing.

The eating of meat had been so deeply ingrained in me that it took me three years to free myself from this habit. Prior to eliminating meat, I had lived with anxiety and insecurity. After fully embracing a plant-based lifestyle, I began to notice myself handling stress with more peace and patience. I have found that following this pathway decreases the mental overload that is felt from all the food choices offered in the market that entice us with convenience but fall short in supporting the wellness of our whole Self.[61]

Ray of Light

The Wisdom Well contains resources and recipes on how to eat more consciously. To get started, try a Ray of Hope Morning Smoothie. Here's the recipe:

Ray of Hope Morning Smoothie

2 cups wild blueberries
1 banana
A handful of organic greens, such as spinach
3 Tbsp organic flaxseed
1 Tbsp of raw honey
4 cups of water
Blend together and enjoy.

Disillusioned with Pharmaceuticals? Try Some Different Tools

"So many people that come to see me and colleagues in my professional network are disillusioned with pharmaceuticals as a long-term solution for trauma and disease," said Kari. "Initial pharmacology is often times needed and welcomed so that the physical body, specifically the central nervous system and neural pathways in the brain, can calm, offering a sense of peace. Yet real peace comes from healing the core, which is possible when one chooses to embark on the journey that releases traumatic imprints from their very essence, with help, ushering in a reframe, reboot, and return to deepened wholeness."

The research of Bessel van der Kolk, MD, author of *The Body Keeps the Score: Brain, Mind, and Body in the Healing of Trauma*, supports and aligns with Kari's wellness philosophies, practices, and observations, with deep connection on how the body truly keeps score of unprocessed emotions and traumatic events. Van der Kolk's reframes healing by linking the brain and disease. In his book, he writes the following:

The brain-disease model overlooks four fundamental truths: (1) our capacity to destroy one another is matched by our capacity to heal one another. Restoring relationships and community is central to restoring well-being; (2) language gives us the power to change ourselves and others by communicating our experiences, helping us to define what we know, and finding a common sense of meaning; (3) we have the ability to regulate our own physiology, including some of the so-called involuntary functions of the body and brain, through such basic activities as breathing, moving, and touching; and (4) we can change social conditions to create environments in which children and adults can feel safe and where they can thrive.

When we ignore these quintessential dimensions of humanity, we deprive people of ways to heal from trauma and restore their autonomy. Being a patient, rather than a participant in one's healing process, separates suffering people from their community and alienates them from an inner sense of self.[62]

Alternative Wellness Tools on the Journey to Wholeness: In Her Own Words, Kari Uselman, PhD

I am grateful for the effective technologies and therapies available today that uplift, entrain, and support a balanced holistic return to well-being. It is truly a divine blessing that two remarkable, intelligently designed devices entered my path and are now an integral part of my holistic wellness practice. Both AmpCoil and quantum biofeedback are key wellness tools for propelling a life-giving shift in my clients on their journey to wholeness.

AmpCoil for emotional upliftment

AmpCoil [a coil used to deliver sound technology that shifts the body's vibration], more than anything else, restored my physical health from Lyme disease and anchored deep peace in my soul, softening the imprint of PTSD from traumatic events. I appreciate the positivity, brain balancing, and harmonizing journeys the system offers, especially for emotional upliftment. It supports physical, emotional, and mental well-being. When the body is in balance, natural healing mechanisms are able to work more efficiently. Since using the AmpCoil, I am no longer light or sound sensitive. I am pain free, joy filled, and can think and remember things with much more ease.

Quantum biofeedback

Back in 2006, I went to a wellness fair in Madison, Wisconsin. Little did I know that as I sat down at the booth, my career was about to change and my soul purpose ignited. The woman behind the table did a quick biofeedback scan and within just a few minutes told me that L4 and L5 in my low back were very stressed (I was recovering from a severe back injury; it was 18 months before I could walk again without pain), and I was showing stress for Hashimoto's hypothyroidism, for which I was just diagnosed. My jaw almost dropped to the floor, as it took MDs over ten years to deduce why I was always so fatigued. There was no way the woman behind the booth could have known about my back or thyroid.

My experiences with quantum biofeedback, from that moment forward, have been remarkable in revealing core stress with my clients as well as delivering stress reduction programs to remind the body of wellness signatures. The INDIGO quantum biofeedback device I use has a PTSD stress-reduction program embedded in the technology. The brainwave and neuro linguistic programs are also wonderful in supporting the reduction of PTSD stress.

The INDIGO Biofeedback System can send signals to measure and record electrophysiological reactions to thousands of items; reeducate certain muscles, nerves, or organs; or it can retrain areas of the body/mind to healthier patterns.

In approximately five minutes, the device can simultaneously detect and record information about the client's stress reactions. The body's reaction to over 11,000 subtle stress-related signatures and physiological parameters are ranked on the main screen to deduce key stress and facilitate cellular balance through running stress-reduction programs along with client education.

If you are feeling lost, I know you can return to a vibrant state with the right support because I did when I felt like nothing and utterly shattered. I believe in you and the power within each of us to overcome. Blessings to you on your journey home to yourself. You are magnificent. You matter. You are worthy. The darkness you may be feeling can lighten. Open, allow, and embrace the beautiful light you are.[63]

Brainspotting

Another alternative therapy is brainspotting. We met with Cherie Lindberg, LPC, who appeared in our film, *Light in the Darkness,* and is the owner of Get Connected Counseling and Consulting. With over twenty years in the human development field, she is a licensed professional counselor, nationally certified counselor, and a Brainspotting trainer and consultant. Because many people aren't familiar with brainspotting, we started the interview by asking some basic questions.

Q: What is brainspotting?

Brainspotting reduces and can eliminate body pain and tension by harnessing the mind and body's natural self-scanning, self-healing ability to dismantle the trauma, distress and beliefs at the subconscious core.

Q: What does brainspotting treat?

Brainspotting treats stress, anxiety, PTSD, sport performance, ADD, dyslexia, emotional blocks, and more. Brainspotting is designed to help people access, process, and overcome trauma, negative emotions, and pain, including psychologically induced physical pain. It is believed that the direction where people look or gaze can affect the way they feel. With this technique, therapists help position the eyes of their clients in ways that allow them to target sources of negative emotions. They use a pointer where they slowly guide the eyes of their clients to find "brainspots." These are eye positions that activate a traumatic memory or painful emotion. When trauma is stored in the body it can change the way our brains work.

Q: Why did you decide to use brainspotting in your thriving therapeutic practice?

I was attracted to brainspotting because, at the core, I want to help people wake up and get connected to themselves and be present. The reason I do this work is that I want people to know that they can heal. So many people give in to that and give up on themselves, and then their whole lives are suffering.

Q: How do you access some of those traumatic memories that are keeping us stuck?

In our subcortical part of our brain, we have blind spots. Our blind spots protect us by keeping traumatic memories pushed down. My client might say, "Hey, I had this memory that happened when I was fifteen," and that's what they think the issue is. Then you start working on that traumatic memory and then all of these other memories that they don't remember can come up too. Sometimes that gets dissociated down there. We teach people how to discharge that out of their central nervous system so that it doesn't become an identity or something that blocks them from achieving something that they want to achieve.

Fishing in the Wisdom Well

Note that insurance coverage of complementary health care approaches can be confusing. Coverage varies depending on state laws, regulations, and your insurance plan. If you are considering trying some of these complementary approaches, check with your health insurance provider first to see whether they will pay for some or all of the treatment.

Using Your Mind, Body, and a Support System to Heal Yourself

Not every therapy has to involve technology, a healing expert, or big out-of-pocket expenses. The common practices of mindfulness, yoga, and relying on a support system can be free or inexpensive ways to heal.

Treating PTSD with Mindfulness

Mindfulness is an ancient Eastern practice popularized in the West by Jon Kabat-Zinn, MD, in the 1970s as a way to reduce stress. Since then, mindfulness has become common practice for many people. Even major universities have mindfulness centers.

Mindfulness is just what it sounds like: being mindful, or aware, of the present moment. The awareness includes not only what is going on around you and what you are thinking, but what you are feeling in your body.

The best part of mindfulness is not judging what we are thinking or feeling or "presencing" but to accept it with kindness and curiosity—and then to give it our loving attention.

Mindfulness takes practice. The more we do it, the better we feel. Plenty of books on the market offer instruction for beginners.

Ray of Light

Have five minutes? Want to give mindfulness a try? You can. Try a meditation app like Headspace or Calm to help relieve stress, anxiety, help you sleep better, and lift your mood, give you happiness, and help boost your hope level. Both offer free trials and provide different options for meditation.

Fishing in the Wisdom Well

Transcendental meditation is a silent, mantra meditation that is sometimes practiced for fifteen to twenty minutes twice per day. It is used for relaxation, stress reduction, and self-development. A recent study suggests that just twenty minutes of meditation twice a day can reduce symptoms of PTSD. The study was conducted on several war veterans in America. After a month of practicing the meditation technique daily, the subjects experienced considerable relief from PTSD symptoms. In fact, the study showed that four out of five veterans were no longer suffering from severe PTSD.[64]

One Breath at a Time: Yoga

It's no secret that yoga can be healing to the mind, body, and soul. It turns out it can be incredibly helpful to people who have experienced trauma in their lives too. There are many different types of yoga practices. Trauma-sensitive yoga teaches people to feel safe within their bodies.

Ray and Janel Norton are owners of Trinity Yoga Studio in New Port Richey, Florida. Ray appeared in our film, *Light in the Darkness*, and shares his story about PTSD and being a first responder. He and his wife are advocates of trauma-informed yoga. They know the power of yoga because they've seen the results in their personal lives and in countless others.

Many people don't give yoga a chance because they have preconceived notions of what someone who practices yoga looks or acts like. We talked to Janel about her yoga practice.

Ray of Light

Yoga has been around for a long time. Yoga originated in ancient India. It's thought to date back to around 3000 BC. It didn't make its way to the Western world until much later—during the late nineteenth and early twentieth centuries.

Much More than Fitness: Janel Norton Shares Her Experience

Yoga is not about how deep into a stretch you can get. They call yoga a practice because there's no end goal to yoga, and it's constantly changing as your body changes.

When I started doing yoga, I did hot power. That was my speed back then. I needed something that was going to engage me and challenge me. I liked it because it exhausted me to the point where I could sleep really well at night. I felt physically strong.

Ray [my husband] would always try to get me into gentle yoga classes, and I'd be like, "I've got an hour to work out. I am not going to waste my time and energy in a classroom sitting there breathing."

Then, I got injured and decided to try the gentle yoga classes, and it was like a completely different mind-set. I was amazed at how calming it was to my nervous system and mind. I was like, "Wow, there's a whole 'nother piece of this yoga practice I've been missing out on."[65]

As a First Responder:
Ray Norton's Surprising Take on Yoga

For me, all throughout my career as a first responder I'm doing a physical job, and I took that part seriously. So, I was always doing cardio at insane levels. I didn't know it at the time, but in the early stages of my career, that was my way of managing stress.

People have preconceived notions of what yoga is, even if they don't know much about it. They might view it as something mystical, being tied to religion or even being just for women. When yoga became more popular in the United States in the 1960s and 1970s, there were certain populations that were drawn to it, like hippies. For fire-fighters and veterans, sometimes there's this whole macho thing about not embracing yoga.

At my first power yoga class I wanted to quit halfway through and there was this lady who was like seventy-five and she was a regular. I couldn't keep up. When the class was done, she got into her car located in the handicap parking spot and put on her oxygen and drove away.

I used to lift heavy weights for years, and I was really strong. I started doing yoga with my wife, Janel, after an injury. I had surgeries on both shoulders. Yoga helped get my flexibility back, and I haven't touched my weights in years.

Today, I am physically and functionally stronger than I've ever been before. As we age, we need to be functionally stronger to get up from a chair. In our studio, we have golfers coming in and they say their game went through the roof after incorporating yoga into their routine.

As a first responder, sometimes I get some eye rolls from the other responders when I mention yoga. But, they give it a try and afterwards they realize how good they feel in their mind and body. You can lift weights all day long, but you're not strengthening all those really important stabilizing muscles that help you get on and off the truck with all that gear on.[66]

Ray of Light

Be adventurous. Check out your local yoga studio or even try a class. Most offer a free trial class to see if you like it. The Nortons note that yoga studios have a different vibe, so don't be afraid to shop around. If you are more comfortable doing yoga from the comfort of your home, there are options there too. Many yoga studios offer live sessions you can stream, or you can even sign up for a program like Peloton where you can stream live or on-demand sessions for all kinds of activities, including yoga. Consider mindfulness to be a practice of paying attention in the present moment. And you do it with intention and without judgment.

What Wellness Looks Like When You Embrace the Whole Person

Ray and Janel know firsthand the importance of supporting the whole person. Their studio offers a variety of yoga classes, and in 2018 they created a wellness center adding massage and counseling services to their thriving yoga studio. Helping those who are dealing with trauma is their biggest passion. That's why they specialize in trauma-informed yoga.

Their instructors have gone through the Warriors at Ease training, which educates yoga instructors on how to work with people who have experienced trauma, including veterans, military personnel, fire fighters, and paramedics. This organization's mission is to bring the power of yoga and meditation to military communities around the world through training, advocacy, programs, and partnerships.

Prior to owning the studio, Janel left her stressful career as a military photojournalist, where she was required to work in war zones. She was attending school working toward her master's degree in strategic communications management. Some of her friends said, "I can see you're really stressed. Why don't you try yoga?" Janel tried hot yoga and was hooked.

"I wish I would have had something like this yoga when I came back from working in a war zone for a few years. And the more I explored that, the more I was like, I just want to know more. I want to know why this works. It's working for me. I want to be able to share this with other people that I know. So, I ended up getting my teacher-training certificate while I was going for my master's degree. I then asked the owners if I could teach a class," said Janel.

In 2016, Janel and Ray purchased the studio. They offer various types of yoga, and all of them are trauma informed so people who come in feel safe.

Dr. Richard Miller is founder, executive director and president of the Integrative Restoration Institute (iRest) as well as a clinical psychologist, author, researcher, yogic scholar, and spiritual teacher. iRest is an evidence-based guided meditation protocol developed at the U.S. Army's Walter Reed Army Hospital. In June of 2010, iRest was endorsed by the U.S. Army Surgeon General and the Defense Center of Excellence as an approved complementary and alternative medicine. iRest is used at over eighty military bases in the United States and Canada and by thousands of people worldwide across diverse populations who are dealing with sleep disorders, PTSD, chemical dependency, chronic pain, depression, anxiety and related disorders.

Janel explains how they use Dr. Miller's work in their studio:

I encourage people that are experiencing trauma, who have PTS or PTSD, to find yoga studios that are trauma informed. In 2006, the U.S. Army's Walter Reed Army Hospital reached out to Dr. Richard Miller, and asked, "Hey, we know the benefits of yoga, but it could trigger people with trauma because of guided imagery leading them to places that wouldn't really be suitable for somebody with trauma." In response, Dr. Miller created a ten-step guided Yoga Nidra protocol that allows those struggling with PTS and PTSD to experience a sense of peace and wholeness within their body and mind.[67]

Fishing in the Wisdom Well

Dr. Lynn Payne's most recent research, "Regenerative Selves: Yoga as a Pedagogy for Cultivating Relationality," supports the conscious healing work Janel and Ray Norton are facilitating with their yoga clients. Yoga cultivates a deep inner awareness. This private piece of self can relate and express to the outer world in a way that is sustainable, regenerative and transformative.

Support Comes in All Forms

Many people isolate when they have a mental illness. But connecting with other people who can relate to your symptoms, is important. It gives us a better, healthier perspective than sitting alone with our thoughts does. Support can come in a group setting (a PTSD support group, for instance) or from a trusted loved one.

Dr. John King Shares the Importance of a Good Support System

I don't think you can recover on your own. Melissa is an important part of my support system. She's only seen me as a man in the process of getting better. Having someone believe in you that much, it drives you to want to get up and do something, drives you to want to get up and make a difference in your life so you can make a difference in their life.

Make sure that you're surrounded with good people. Anything you face, you've got a team of people with you that are going to help you overcome it. That group of people that you do trust, that's essential to healing from something like post-traumatic stress.

Everyone needs someone who will see them, see them trying. You need to have those people in your life that love you. Good or bad, they don't want anything from you, they just love you and they want to see you grow beyond where you are. I think that's absolutely vital for success.[68]

Mike Vaessen Shares Why Support Is So Important

If I had swept it under the rug and not had a good network of people to talk to, I possibly could've gone the opposite way and just gotten deeper and deeper. I was not doing myself any favors by shutting all the drapes, playing computer games, watching TV, eating too many Doritos, and drinking too much beer. Thank God I had all my friends and neighbors and family. If you just sit on your own, it's not going to help you. You need to talk to people.[69]

Thank you for taking this journey with us. We appreciate it and most of all we hope you've learned something new and most of all have *hope* and feel the support of those who love you.

Note all the resources listed here can be accessed on https://Consciouscontent.org by clicking on the Wisdom Well Resources link.

THE WISDOM WELL

Reading:

Myss, Caroline. *Anatomy of the Spirit: Seven Stages to Power and Healing.* NY: Harmony, 1996. Building on wisdom from Hindu, Christian, and Kaballah traditions, this comprehensive guide to energy healing reveals the hidden stresses, beliefs, and attitudes that cause illness.

Gerber, Richard, M.D. *Vibrational Medicine: The #1 Handbook of Subtle Energy Therapies.* Rochester, VT: Bear & Company. 2001. Dr. Gerber (1954-2007) was trained both in conventional Western medicine as well as alternative therapies. This book provides an encyclopedic overview on energetic healing treatments, covering subtle-energy fields, homeopathy, radionics, electrotherapy, meditation and more.

Pfeiffer, Carl Curt. *Nutrition and Mental Illness: An Orthomolecular Approach to Balancing Body Chemistry.* Rochester, VT, Vermont: Healing Arts Press, 1987. There is beautiful wisdom in the research and suggested nutritional additions presented in this book. Dr. Pfeifer's nutritional protocols hope to those seeking a holistic long-term healing process. When followed consistently, efficacy is maintained.

Yu, Simon, MD, *Accidental Cure: Extraordinary medicine for Extraordinary Patients.* St. Louis, MO: Preventions and Healing, Inc. 2010. Dr. Yu has learned to use energy medicine as a new biometric diagnostic technique and is a leading medical doctor and clinician who merges Western medical science with Eastern medical philosophy, His book explores the connection between quantum physics ad biocybernetics and five therapies that address the core of disease which include parasite elimination, detoxing heavy metals, detecting and removing hidden dental infections, resolving food allergies and nutrition and dietary support to assist a return to wellness. He offers examples, stories, and solutions. This is a fabulous book that goes beyond sedating a symptom to understanding and remediating core stressors so that one truly heals and returns to wholeness.

Williams, Anthony. *Life-Changing Foods: Save Yourself and the Ones You Love with the Hidden Healing Powers of Fruits & Vegetables.* Carlsbad, CA: Hay House, 2016. This book shows how you can treat dozens of illnesses with targeted healing regimens in which nutrition plays a major role. It delves deeper into the healing power of over 50 fruits, vegetables, herbs and spices, and wild foods that can have an extraordinary effect on health. Anthony explains each food's properties, the symptoms and conditions it can help relieve or heal, and the emotional and spiritual benefits it brings. And he offers delicious recipes to help you enjoy each food's maximum benefit, from sweet potatoes with braised cabbage stuffing to honey-coconut ice cream.

Engelhart, Terces. *I Am Grateful: Recipes and Lifestyle of Cafe Gratitude.* Berkeley, CA: North Atlantic Books, 2007. With locations in San Francisco, Berkeley, Marin, and Los Angeles, Café Gratitude has become well known for its inspiring environment and distinctive, flavorful organic foods. In *I Am Grateful*, cofounder Terces Engelhart presents her and her husband Matthew's view of life and business philosophy. She also presents her story of personal healing, sharing highlights of her recovery from food addiction while explaining the benefits of a raw lifestyle. Recipes include café favorites such as the "I Am Luscious" raw chocolate smoothie, "I Am Bountiful" bruschetta, "I Am

Elated" spicy rolled enchiladas, and "I Am Amazing" lemon meringue pie with macadamia nut crust.

Cousens, Gabriel. *Rainbow Green Live-Food Cuisine.* Berkeley: CA: North Atlantic Books, 2003. Both a guide to natural health and a cookbook, it features over 250 revolutionary vegan recipes from chefs at the Tree of Life Cafe, from Buttery Butternut Porridge to Raw-violis to Carob Coconut Cream Eclairs. Combining modern research on metabolism, ecological consciousness, and a rainbow of live foods, Dr. Cousens dishes up comprehensive, practical, and delectable solutions to the woes of the Western diet.

Zinckenko, David. *Eat This, Not That: The Best Foods in America.* NY: Ballentine Books, 2019. Shows you how to eat healthier with simple food swaps—whether you're dining in or out—is now expanded and completely updated.

Watching/Listening:

Using Brainspotting to Connect to Higher Self. (5:04) Therapist and Brainspotting Trainer and Consultant, Cherie Lindberg, explains how to use this technique to connect to your best self (Higher Self) on your own.

What is Brainspotting? (4:03) Therapist and Brainspotting Trainer and Consultant, Cherie Lindberg, uses brainspotting on a client.

Healy - Frequencies for Life. Healy is a wearable device containing frequency programs that help promote your health, vitality and overall wellbeing. It is a microcurrent medical device that has only been cleared by the U.S. Food and Drug Administration for local relief of acute, chronic, and arthritis pain and muscle soreness due to overexertion. Healy also has non-medical applications that use individualized frequencies to help balance your mind and body and relieve stress.

Taking Action:

Visit PTSD Alliance which shares helpful resources to find treatment in your area

ACOG offers a 24 Hour Hotline for women in abusive situations.

ADAA links to a PTSD mobile coaching app (from the US Department of Veteran Affairs).

ADAA provides a directory of local mental health professionals.

ADAA lets you search for PTSD support groups in your area, or walks you through the steps to start your own support group.

ISTSS provides a Clinician Directory that allows you to search for a mental health professional based on your location, doctor specialty, special interests, demographic, and language.

Sidran Institute offers a Help Desk to find personalized, compassionate support.

Looking for a therapist who specializes in ART? Locate one here.

Visit War Heroes for Horses. Horses are amazing creatures and can easily sense emotions of humans. War Horses for Heroes is a non-profit organization that provides equine-assisted therapy to veterans who have sustained service-related mental or physical injuries.

Visit the National Alliance on Mental Illness Helpline which is a free service that provides information, referrals and support to people living with a mental health condition, family members and caregivers, mental health providers and the public.

Look into joining a PTSD clinical trial just like Veteran Tony Seahorn did. You can be part of tomorrow's medical breakthroughs. NIMH researchers across the United States conduct many studies. Visit the NIMH Clinical Trials page to learn how. To learn the basics about clinical trials, check out NIMH's Clinical Research Trials and You: Questions and Answers brochure.

Check out the Brainspotting.com website to learn more about how brainspotting started and how it is used effectively in therapy. Also includes information on becoming certified.

Consider setting up an appointment with therapist and Brainspotting Trainer and Practitioner Cherie Lindberg to explore brainspotting at her therapeutic practice, Get Connected Counseling and Consulting.

To explore mindfulness consider signing up for Headspace, an app to help you with meditation in 3 minutes. They claim in 10 days you can increase happiness by 16%. You can try it for free.

Want to stress less and sleep better? If so, explore the Calm app, you can even try it for free.

Request to join Spiritual Wisconsin Facebook group. This is a group for people knowingly on a journey or those just learning why they are here on earth. We are on a journey in this life together. Here you can post, learn about events to improve your knowledge or intuition.

Check out apps like Daylio that track your moods and other variables such as exercise, sleep, nutrition, and socialization or hobbies so that you can gain insight about correlations such as your moods being very much connected to your menstrual cycle or your nutrition so you can address these issues.

Consider joining a Twelve Step group for increased awareness and support around any issues with which you are struggling. There are nearly 40 different Twelve Step groups or fellowships out there including Co-Dependents Anonymous, Al-Anon, Debtors Anonymous, and Sex and Love Addicts Anonymous. Meetings are free and meetings are also available online.

Learn more about sprouting at Sprout People, which serves the home sprouter. They have a passion for encouraging people to grow their own food. They are committed to making your sprouting experience as perfect as possible, so in addition to the most extensive list of seeds anywhere, they offer a wide range of sprouters and other tools, thorough growing instructions, recipes and complete "technical support".

Discover more about AmpCoil at www.AmpCoil.com. The AmpCoil system is more than a device, it's an opportunity to transform yourself and your loved ones through vibration. In a world where technology is pervasive, their aim is to harness the benefits of sound technology to shift your vibration toward a state of wellness.

Discover more about quantum biofeedback and its healing qualities.

CONCLUSION

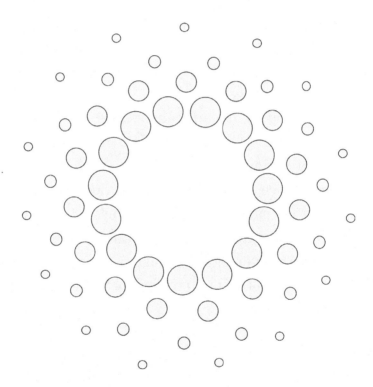

You are a light in the darkness.

-Kimberly Resch and Brian Ross

Thank you for taking this journey with us. Writing this book was not easy. It was a difficult task in itself to come to terms with our personal struggles. Sharing them with the world seemed like an insurmountable goal but has proven to be the next big step in our healing journey.

We acknowledge there are life experiences that leave a lasting positive or negative impression. If we allow them to do so, they can change our internal compass toward the light. Acknowledging our true self and self-reflection are powerful tools that dictate our output to the world.

In this book, you have read many stories of intimate experiences and pain, followed by hope. You may have witnessed hope getting up in the morning with the sunrise as it's a new chance to make a different decision. You have the power to decide your fate. No one's journey is quite the same. As humans, we have an innate ability to withstand the most adverse of circumstances and still prosper. Our hope for you is that you recognize you are already the brightest shining star.

When you face a difficult life challenge, it's that fork in the road where you have to choose whether to stay on the same road in that pain, suffering, and negativity or turn onto a new path. The new path may allow you to find purpose moving forward to propel you into what is, in fact, your "real" life. Be clear about your intention. We can sometimes fall prey to living this life for someone else, which may not be your highest benefit.

We chose a new path when we went through the heartbreaking and challenging loss of losing our child, Taylor. Taylor's tragic and unexpected death changed everything and forced us to decide whether to fall heavily into the sorrow that was becoming our new reality or find meaning in it. Taylor would not have wanted us to give up. He was now a bright light needed to illuminate our passion and turn that into our purposeful mission.

For me, Kimberly, Taylor is one of my daily inspirations. I feel sad a lot and miss having those awesome, almost daily conversations about goals and accomplishments. His voice is ingrained in my head as he reminds me, "I got this." He would tell me how much he loved watching his mom accomplish her dreams and goals no matter how crazy they were. We would conspire together to create plans and action steps that would help him accomplish his dreams. He was unstoppable, a trait I hope he got from me.

I feel Taylor smiling so big; I honor his legacy by building mine. I am sending everyone love and healing energy as you work through life looking through your possibility lens. Your battles will be lessons of strength as you continue to do the "good work" in this life. We need more of that. You are a "Light in the Darkness," and I see you.

NOTES

INTRODUCTION

1. Brent Bezo and Stefania Maggi, "Living in 'survival mode:' Intergenerational transmission of trauma from the Holodomor genocide of 1932–1933 in Ukraine," *Social Science & Medicine* 134 (2015): 87-94. https://www.sciencedirect.com/science/article/abs/pii/S0277953615002294.

2. Brent Bezo and Stefania Maggi, "Intergenerational perceptions of mass trauma's impact on physical health and well-being," *Psychological Trauma: Theory, Research, Practice, and Policy* 10, no. 1 (2018): 87–94. https://doi.org/10.1037/tra0000284.

3. Támara Hill, "Inter-generational Trauma: 6 Ways it Affects Families," *Psych Central*, June 5, 2018, https://blogs.psychcentral.com/caregivers/2018/06/inter-generational-trauma-6-ways-it-affects-families/.

4. Patrick Obissier, *Biogenealogy: Decoding the Psychic Roots of Illness: Freedom from the Ancestral Origins of Disease* (Rochester, VT: Healing Arts Press, 2006).

5. Patrick Obissier, *Biogenealogy: Decoding the Psychic Roots of Illness: Freedom from the Ancestral Origins of Disease* (Rochester, VT: Healing Arts Press, 2006).

6. Enrique Bouron, "Total Biology of All Living Things and Biological Decoding." *Enrique Bouron*, 2020. http://www.bouron.net/BiologiaTotal.

7. Christian Flèche. *The Biogenealogy Sourcebook: Healing the Body by Resolving Traumas of the Past* (Rochester, VT: Healing Arts Press, 2008).

8. Enrique Bouron, "Total Biology of All Living Things and Biological Decoding." *Enrique Bouron*, 2020. http://www.bouron.net/BiologiaTotal.

9. Ryke Geerd Hamer, "German New Medicine," *German New Medicine*, 2000, https://learninggnm.com/.

10. Christian Flèche. *The Biogenealogy Sourcebook: Healing the Body by Resolving Traumas of the Past* (Rochester, VT: Healing Arts Press, 2008).

11. "About the CDC - Kaiser ACE Study," *Centers for Disease Control and Prevention*, April 13, 2020, https://www.cdc.gov/violenceprevention/acestudy/about.html.

12. "Got Your ACE Score?" *ACEs Too High,* accessed 2020, https://acestoohigh.com/got-your-ace-score/.

13. "ACE Study," *ACEs Too High*, July 22, 2020, https://acestoohigh.com/category/ace-study/.

14. Candace Pert, *Molecules of Emotion: Why You Feel the Way You Feel* (New York: Simon & Schuster, 2012).

PART I

15. "Study: Police Officers and Firefighters Are More Likely to Die by Suicide than in Line of Duty," *Ruderman Family Foundation*, accessed 2020,

https://rudermanfoundation.org/white_papers/police-offi-cers-and-firefighters-are-more-likely-to-die-by-suicide-than-in-line-of-duty/.

16. "Post-Traumatic Stress Disorder," *National Institute of Mental Health*, May 2019, https://www.nimh.nih.gov/health/topics/post-traumatic-stress-disorder-ptsd/index.shtml#:~:tex-t=Anyone%20can%20develop%20PTSD%20at,some%20point%20in%20their%20lives.

17. "Posttraumatic Stress Disorder," *National Alliance on Mental Illness*, December 2017, https://www.nami.org/About-Mental-Illness/Mental-Health-Conditions/Posttraumatic-Stress-Disorder.

18. "How Common is PTSD in Adults?" *U.S. Department of Veterans Affairs*, accessed 2020, https://www.ptsd.va.gov/under-stand/common/common_adults.asp.

19. "PTSD Canada Has the Highest Rate, Plus Eight More Sur-prising Facts," *Canadian Broadcasting Corporation*, accessed 2020, https://www.cbc.ca/natureofthings/features/ptsd-canada-has-the-highest-rate-and-other-surprising-things.

20. "Posttraumatic Stress Disorder," *National Alliance on Mental Illness*, December 2017, https://www.nami.org/About-Mental-Illness/Mental-Health-Conditions/Posttraumatic-Stress-Disorder.

21. Ray Norton, interview by Brian Ross and Kimberly Resch, *Light in the Darkness*, Conscious Content, LLC, 2018.

22. Mike Vaessen, interview by Brian Ross and Kimberly Resch, *Light in the Darkness*, Conscious Content, LLC, 2018.

23. Tony Seahorn, interview by Brian Ross and Kimberly Resch, *Light in the Darkness*, Conscious Content, LLC, 2018.

24. World Health Organization, *Guidelines for medico-legal care for victims of sexual violence* (Geneva: World Health Organization Publications, 2003). https://apps.who.int/iris/bitstream/handle/10665/42788/924154628X.pdf;jsessionid =7BD9741D59A5C0FD1EC17FF79CBC2705?sequence=1.

25. Melissa T. Merrick et al. "Vital Signs: Estimated Proportion of Adult Health Problems Attributable to Adverse Childhood Experiences and Implications for Prevention—25 States, 2015–2017," *Centers for Disease Control and Prevention Morbidity and Mortality Weekly Report* 68, no. 44 (2019): 999. https://www.cdc.gov/mmwr/volumes/68/wr/mm6844e1.htm#:~:text=The%20 estimated%20overall%20percentage%20reductions,and%20 heavy%20drinking%20(23.9%25).

26. John King, interview by Brian Ross and Kimberly Resch, *Light in the Darkness*, Conscious Content, LLC, 2018.

27. Janet Seahorn, interview by Corrine Casanova, March 16, 2020.

28. "Screening for Posttraumatic Stress Disorder (PTSD)," *Anxiety and Depression Association of America*, accessed 2020, https://adaa.org/screening-posttraumatic-stress-disorder-ptsd.

29. Janet Seahorn, interview by Corrine Casanova, March 16, 2020.

30. Janet Seahorn, interview by Corrine Casanova, March 16, 2020.

31. Matthew J. Friedman, "PTSD History and Overview," *U.S. Department of Veterans Affairs*, accessed 2020, https://www.ptsd.va.gov/professional/treat/essentials/history_ptsd.asp#:~:text=In%201980%2C%20the%20American%20Psychiatric,in%20 psychiatric%20theory%20and%20practice.

32. Janet Seahorn, interview by Corrine Casanova, March 16, 2020.

33. Jayne Leonard, "What to know about complex PTSD," *Medical News Today*, August 28, 2018, https://www.medicalnewstoday.com/articles/322886#symptoms.

34. Jennifer Jamison, interview by Corrine Casanova, March 11, 2020.

35. Jack Kornfield, "How Mindfulness Can Break the Cycle of Fear and Anger," *National Institute for Clinical Application of Behavioral Medicine*, accessed 2020, https://www.nicabm.com/overcoming-fear/.

36. Claire Gecewicz, "'New Age' beliefs common amongst both religious and non-religious Americans," *Pew Research Center*, October 1, 2018, https://www.pewresearch.org/fact-tank/2018/10/01/new-age-beliefs-common-among-both-religious-and-nonreligious-americans/.

37. DeEtte Ranae, interview by Corrine Casanova on March 18, 2020.

38. "Prayer for People with PTSD," *Patience Mason's PTSD Blog*, June 28, 2014, http://patiencemason.blogspot.com/2014/06/y-28-of-national-ptsd-awareness-month.html?m=0.

PART II

39. *Unlocking Us with Brené Brown*, episode five, "David Kessler and Brené on Grief and Finding Meaning," performed by Brené Brown and David Kessler, aired March 30, 2020, podcast.

40. David Kessler, *Finding Meaning: The Sixth Stage of Grief* (New York: Scribner, 2019).

41. Nathalie Himmelrich, *Grieving Parents: Surviving Loss as a Couple* (Kat Biggie Press, 2014).

42. Deborah Spungen, *And I Don't Want to Live This Life: A Mother's Story of Her Daughter's Murder* (New York: Ballantine Books, 1996).

43. McQuillan, Susan, "11 Ways Plants Enhance Your Mental and Emotional Health." *Psychology Today*. September 14, 2019. https://www.psychologytoday.com/us/blog/cravings/201909/11-ways-plants-enhance-your-mental-and-emotional-health.

44. Tiffany Anderson, interview by Corrine Casanova, June 10, 2020.

PART III

45. Sandy Walden, interview by Kimberly Resch, August 15, 2020.

46. John King, interview by Brian Ross and Kimberly Resch, *Light in the Darkness*, Conscious Content, 2018.

47. Jennifer Sweeton, *Trauma Treatment Toolbox: 165 Brain-Changing Tips, Tools & Handouts to Move Therapy Forward* (Eau Claire: PESI Publishing, 2019).

48. Daniel Amen, "Change Your Brain, Change Your Life." 2011, Orange County, CA, TEDxOrangeCoast, 19:10. https://www.youtube.com/watch?v=MLKj1puoWCg&list=PLeUloVnGorc5WiM3khaQUOvkPeik1qtUO&index=20.

49. Kerstin Uvnäs-Moberg et al, "Self-soothing behaviors with particular reference to oxytocin release induced by non-noxious sensory stimulation," *Frontiers in Psychology* 5, no. 1529 (2014). https://www.ncbi.nlm.nih.gov/pmc/articles/PMC4290532/.

50. Deanna Culver, interview by Corrine Casanova, May 4, 2020.

51. "Mental Health Conditions," *National Alliance on Mental Illness,* accessed 2020, https://www.nami.org/Learn-More/Mental-Health-Conditions.

PART IV

52. Margaret Nagib, "The Power and Science of Hope," *MindWise Innovations,* accessed 2020, https://www.mindwise.org/blog/community/the-power-and-science-of-hope/.

53. Harold G. Koenig, "Religion, spirituality, and health: the research and clinical implications," *ISRN Psychiatry,* 2012, https://www.ncbi.nlm.nih.gov/pubmed/23762764.

54. Stoerkel, Ericka, "Can Random Acts of Kindness Increase Well-Being?" *Positive Psychology.* April 7, 2019. https://positivepsychology.com/random-acts-kindness/.

55. Paul S. Mueller et al, "Religious Involvement, Spirituality, and Medicine," *Mayo Clinic Proceedings* 76 (2001): 1225-1235. https://www.mayoclinicproceedings.org/article/S0025-6196(11)62799-7/pdf.

56. Annah Pelot, interview by Corrine Casanova, August 20, 2020.

PART V

57. Kari Uselman, interview by Corrine Casanova, August 22, 2020.

58. Scott Bill, interview by Brian Ross and Kimberly Resch, *Light in the Darkness,* Conscious Content, 2018.

LIGHT IN THE DARKNESS

59. Kari Uselman, interview by Corrine Casanova, August 20, 2020.

60. Annah Pelot, interview by Corrine Casanova, August 22, 2020.

61. Annah Pelot, interview by Corrine Casanova, August 19, 2020.

62. Bessel van der Kolk, *The Body Keeps the Score: Brain, Mind, and Body in the Healing of Trauma* (New York: Penguin Books, 2014).

63. Kari Uselman, interview by Corrine Casanova, August 22, 2020.

64. "Meditating twice a day for 20 mins cut PTSD symptoms in older adults," *Asian News International*, January 14, 2018, https://www.aninews.in/news/health/meditating-twice-a-day-for-20-mins-cut-ptsd-symptoms-in-older-adults201801141557260002/.

65. Janel Norton, interview by Corrine Casanova, May 15, 2020.

66. Ray Norton, interview by Corrine Casanova, May 15, 2020.

67. "iRest Institute," *iRest,* accessed 2020, https://www.irest.org/.

68. John King, interview by Brian Ross and Kimberly Resch, *Light in the Darkness,* Conscious Content, 2018.

69. Mike Vaessen, interview by Brian Ross and Kimberly Resch, *Light in the Darkness,* Conscious Content, 2018.

ACKNOWLEDGMENTS

This book is the culmination of divine timing and connection. We started this project with one intention and then, as life does, everything we knew was interrupted. The mystery of life unfolded as we dove into the subject matter. It was our life weaving into the tapestry of others being called to participate in a time of remote darkness. We bared our souls on paper. A few chosen by the grace of God rose up even in their own uncomfortability to share, research, acknowledge and write with us in real time to capture the essence of our message to you the reader. We have been blessed and honored to have shared space with these lovely energies.

First and foremost, we are humbled by the tragic loss of our vibrant light, Taylor. We now belong to the club no one wants to belong to. As we progress each day, we acknowledge he has been a massive catalyst to share the intimate details of our experience thus relating to so many with stories of their own to provide healing modalities to facilitate a positive shift to alleviate the pressure of our reality.

The series of events that have happened since this book became a reality have blessed us beyond our imagination. The people listed below are the foundation of this work.

Our Co-writer Corrine Casanova

What a journey we have taken together these last nine months. Thank you so much for taking on such a big project, not really knowing what you were getting yourself into. Between the pandemic and a tragic loss and the redirection of this transcript, you hung in there with us as we were all trying to figure out what was going to happen. It was magical how all of us showed up during this adversity and really made something beautiful together to share. We love your zest for learning and your sweet demeanor. Thank you so much for your guidance, partnership, and for being the best editor and friend to us. We love you and send you good energy every day!

Our Friend and Partner

To my dearest friend, Dick, thank you for your support and love during this tragic loss. Calling to check on me and listening when I needed to talk has been so helpful. My heart is so grateful for you. So many things have become possible because you are in my life. Please know that the divine chance meeting we had four years ago with you listening to a girl who was trying to make a difference in the world, really came true with hard work and dedication.

I am beyond grateful for your continued support of the Conscious Content mission. Please know your legacy has made ours possible. Myself and our team are sending you so many blessings.

Our Companion Animals

To our life partners, our ride or die boxer dogs. Our gratitude extends to Phoenix and Apollo for being our companions and holding space for us as we wrote, researched, and pondered the meaning of life 18 hours a day in the last 30 day stretch to complete this insurmountable task with our team. They provided us breaks by demanding our attention to have fun several times a day, especially in times where we were feeling grief and pain. They made us laugh as we rode in golf carts while they hunted for bunnies froliced in the flooded meadows after the Florida thunderstorms on Lake Okeechobee. There was so much joy in their actions every second as they slept, played, and snacked with us each day. They gifted us moments of balance and provided us the energy to complete this task with hope. They asked for hugs when we needed them. Phoenix and Apollo remind us to find joy in simply being present.

Our Moms

Grace Ross and Dawn Carlson who have been the most important energies in our lives, for without them we wouldn't be here. They are the bringers of lessons, high standards, joy, support along our journey, and are ultimately responsible for forging us into who we are today. They have taught us to lead by example using the basic principles of self reliance and fortitude, just as they did before us.

My Mom (Kimberly)

To my mom Dawn, thank you for choosing me as your child. I am sure being my mom was no easy task. I'm certain raising a headstrong, overachieving daughter almost caused PTS. Your resilience and determination for quality work taught me by example to never half-ass anything. Reminding me along the way that if I am going to put my most prized commodity of time into anything, I need to do it to the best of my ability every time.

I appreciate your video chats reminding me that even though writing this book is so hard emotionally, it was a book that would relate to so many and it needed to be finished with grace. Thank you for taking such good care of our grown kids after they moved up north after Taylor died. That made this process easier as a mom, knowing they have you nearby to watch over them. I know you keep an eye on them and keep them in lefsa, home cooked meals, and your prized banana bread. Most importantly, I am so proud of your ability to manage me throughout my life and hold me to the highest of standards, including when it came to something as important as writing this book. I will continue to pay it forward. I think that is the best gift you have given me. I love you.

My Mom (Brian)

To my mom Grace, first let me say thank you for managing the house while we were away writing this book. It was immensely helpful and allowed for less stress knowing things were handled. Secondly, I know parenting me after dad died was not easy or for the faint of heart. I am sure that I stressed you out of your mind as a teen, we can just refer to the stories I shared in this book. I know you have done the best you could and have been my biggest fan while motivating me to work hard through both my big successes and my setbacks. As a "Grama," you were always there for Morgan and Ashlee with a sweet smile and good attitude. I appreciate you helping get them to dance classes or wherever they needed to be over the years. I appreciate that you have never judged me and always offered to help through my difficult divorce. I know you loved and cared about her and that was probably tough. Thank you, Mom. I love you.

My Kids (Kimberly)

To my first born Cody, I honor your capacity to love with all of your heart. You are an amazing and protective big brother to Zach and Taylor. I want to thank you for loving them so hard and making them a priority in your life even as an adult. Although we are all beings in healing progress, I am sincerely grateful that you have found the capacity to begin to work through the loss of your little brother. I pray that you find peace and the energy to be in a state of gratitude for all that you are and all that you have become for your kids. You have evolved so much as a person. You and Raelyn are amazing parents to Kairi and Orion, and I send you all blessings every day for you to find joy, peace, and healing. I love you. Zoot Zoot.

My dearest Zachary, my most sensitive Soul. I am so encouraged by your healing path and appreciate that you know this life takes work to get where you want to go. Healing from a huge loss like Taylor has taken its toll, and I hope this book can be a legacy that you'll be proud of. Thank you so much for your contribution and research in this book. I appreciate your can-do attitude and the diligence to get the tasks done in a timely manner. Thank you for taking such extraordinary care of Jasper, our fur baby. As your mom, I just want to say how proud of you I am and tell you how smart you are. It's really exciting to have a child that shares your vision and is passionate about helping and healing the world. I love to watch you learn and grow. Thank you for all that you do for Conscious Content. I love you! Zoot Zoot!

Andrew (Taylor's dad)

Dearest Andrew, I don't know where to begin in apologizing for what happened to Taylor. My heart is so heavy for our loss. He was the most beautiful human being. I am sending you love and healing energy. I hope you continue to find the strength to move through the grieving process and be patient with yourself. I am so proud of you and appreciative of your handling of this delicate experience with kindness and love towards me. My heart is so grateful for that. Thank you for taking such exceptional care of Taylor when you had him. He was a lucky boy to have you in his corner everyday. I am sending you blessings for a purposeful life and the continued healing for yourself.

My Kids (Brian)

To my daughter Morgan, this last year has been a pivotal year for many of us, and watching you evolve beyond trauma and understanding the importance of self-care has been an inspiration and a personal motivation for me. You were my buddy as a young child and I miss spending that time with you. I am so proud of who you are becoming as a young adult as you venture out on your own. I know that you loved Taylor as your brother and that his unexpected passing affected you very deeply. Your drive to heal and desire to live your best life is amazing to witness. I love connecting with you during our many FaceTime calls. Thank you for contributing to our book with the hope quotes you selected, they were perfect. We have discussed that life is a choice and my hope for you is that you will use your light to shine bright in this world. You are a special person and you have a beautiful life ahead of you. I love you with all of my being, Dad.

To my daughter Ashlee, as a child you were always confident. Your bright eyes and sweet smile could light up a room. I love your drive to excel and appreciate your ability to decompress when necessary. I have always tried my best to be a dad you could look up to and feel safe with. I want to lead by example and leave a legacy you can be proud of. Over the years, you have blossomed as a person who cares deeply for the people you love. You have grown into a beautiful young lady. I know the last three years have been difficult for you with so much change. Thank you for being patient with me as we figure it all out.

My hope for you is that you continue to find your voice because I know how powerful you are inside. I cannot wait to see what's possible for you as an adult. I love you and cherish the time I have with you, Dad.

Sonya (Morgan and Ashlee's mom)

Thank you Sonya for sharing all of the good memories and all of the challenging times. Somewhere along the road of life, we lost our way through all the ups and downs. I have learned so much over the course of nearly 30 years with you. Most importantly, I have learned that to know ourselves, who we really are, is the best gift we can give to our girls. They are in this world finding their place and searching for meaning. As we find it ourselves, we live by example and leave a legacy we all can be proud of.

Our Spiritual Directors

Kari Uselman, PhD and Annah Pelot

We want to thank you both from a special place in our hearts and Souls. Our lives have come full circle together again to manifest and create profound things. We call it doing the "good work."

Your energies are infused within these pages as we performed miracles together in the last days of writing the chapters of this book. What a remarkable process to be a part of. We know that this transcript evolved into what it has become because of this group effort. Thank you both for joining our family again to help us leave this legacy to the world.

Daily House Publishing

We would like to thank and recognize our family at Daily House Publishing. The outstanding team of Kitty, Corrine, Alexanne, Kate, and Jenn has given us an exceptional experience for our first book. You helped us develop, plan, and build the confidence we needed to begin the difficult task of writing a book that was useful, interesting, and profound. Along this journey, we experienced the worst kind of tragedy and wondered whether or not we had it in us to continue with the work and complete this book on schedule. Thank you for having an open mind about us completely changing the book's narrative while always supporting us and keeping us on task until this remarkable book was completed. Also, thank you to our book designer, Andrea, for her creativity, hard work, and dedication.

Shaman Motion Pictures

This book was inspired by the film we created together. Josh, Dan, and Mark, you guys are our family. We are so grateful for your cinematic genius and ability to tell the story we had in our head to the world in such a beautiful way for *Light in the Darkness*. Thank you for being such excellent partners for so many years and on so many projects, we love you guys. We send you blessings and increased success and prosperity, always!

Max Hauser Media

Max, you may be one of the most talented artistic cinematographers I've ever met. Thank you for being a grinder and for taking my calls and texts at all hours of the day. Thank you for taking the extra care and time to help us to find our voice with so many projects, including this one. The film "book" trailers you created were stunning.

Smith Publicity

A big thanks to our publicity company for taking us to the next level of awareness in this world! Thank you for believing in our mission and helping us heal the world and spread light.

Light in the Darkness Contributors

John King, Ph.D.

Linda Bell

Ardelia Bell

Cherie Lindberg, LPC

Kari Uselman, Ph.D.

Annah Pelot

Tony Seahorn

Janet Seahorn, Ph.D.

Kathysue Dorey

Ray Norton

Janel Norton

Mike Vaessen

Jennifer Jamison

DeEtte Ranae

Sandy Walden

Deanna Culver

Khristi Kennedy Otto, DC

Tiffany Anderson

Kathryn Pollack

Nikki Davis

Our Review Panel

Thank you for those who have taken the time to read our manuscript and provide feedback. We appreciate you.

Marie Green

Dawn Carlson

Brett Hensley

Paul Linzmeyer

Judy Green

Anjali Seefeldt, MA, CBFA

Amanda Rudd

Corey Torres

Sasha Mauck

Sandy Walden

Jennifer Duquette

Khristi Kennedy Otto, DC

Marcella Raymond

Dwight Bain

Jarvis Johnson

Lisa Kelly

ACKNOWLEDGMENTS

Jim Etzin

Kathy Velasquez

Jeffrey Veal

Gabi Ruggieri

Illustrations:

Kimberly Resch

Additional Research:

Morgan Ross

Zachary Ericksen

Jacob Bowman

ABOUT THE AUTHORS

About Brian Ross

Brian's experience is rooted in business and the philosophy of servant leadership, which has been one of the most important aspects of his output to the world. Conscious Content was created in this space of gratitude and service with his partner Kimberly Resch. One of the more interesting facts about Brian's leadership style is for him to lead by example and hold himself and everyone in his organization to the standard of "remarkable." This required being present, listening more than talking, and feeling what the next, right move is for his organization.

Within this space, Conscious Content has manifested multiple awards for its feature films and short films in connection with Shaman Motion Pictures. These films have left an imprint of education and awareness to those who watch them. Now adding "author" to his long list of accomplishments, the book "Light in the Darkness: Uncovering Grief and Trauma" was a labor of love in every way. Created during the most unprecedented time in history for us, forging ahead with this message was imperative. It was necessary for this experience to be laid in the same foundation, as always, with one caveat of loss leading his journey this time.

Understanding that grief and trauma happen to nearly every person he connected with, there seemed to be a need for a positive experience while going through the healing process. "Light in the Darkness" was born and is a project that he is really proud of and excited to share with others. Everyone has experiences worth sharing, and in his newest life chapter as "author," he took the deepest dive into himself and shared space with others willing to do the same. This resulted in showing us the "how", the "why" and the "what" we may gain from knowledge and experience from others during our life journey.

About Kimberly Resch

Kimberly has lived a pretty interesting life so far, as some might say. Starting off as a creative at the age of 5, winning awards for artwork, then expanding that passion into selling original works of art for top dollar at the age of 16, she has channeled her creative flow into another work of art in film and has now added "author" to her list of accomplishments. As a Shaman in the British West Indies and British Overseas Territory, Kimberly was of service to those on a healing path.

Rooted in truth and self-awareness, her extensive education in EIQ (emotional intelligence quotient) has served her clients well in discovering the root causes of dis-ease in their body, mind, and spirit. Although her practical experience in corporate life provided for her family financially, she acknowledged that the "human" arts are the foundation of her passion. Building the world-class organization, Conscious Content, with her partner Brian Ross over the last several years has given herself and others a place for those who need a voice to be heard on issues that matter to humanity.

Her time as an "author" has been the most challenging and healing experience for Kimberly so far. The writing was easy, the recalling of sensitive experiences was not. After the significant loss of losing her 15-year-old son to a drowning phenomenon called "shallow water blackout" in March of 2020, it's been necessary for Kimberly to find her voice to help others experiencing grief and trauma. There is a unique process of grieving and working through the experience of loss that is like a fingerprint for each person. The goal is to #liftthestigma and create a "light in the darkness" while uncovering grief and trauma in our lives. The book and complementary film of the same name feature her best efforts with experts and survivors featured in this work to convey this important message. We must work through it and remember that "hope" is the most important ingredient along our journey.

About Corrine Casanova

Corrine has been fascinated with people's stories ever since she can remember. Sharing stories is one of the big reasons she chose to pursue a Journalism degree at the University of Minnesota. Her passion for books started early. She was *that* kid who went to the Bookmobile (a portable library on wheels) and came home with a stack of books to read each week.

For 20 years, she has been helping authors write books. She's held editing and management positions with traditional book publishers and most recently joined Daily House, LLC, a book publishing services company that specializes in providing authors the care and guidance that you expect from a traditional publisher but without the loss of royalties or artistic control. When she's not helping authors craft their next bestseller, she enjoys being active outdoors. She enjoys running, hiking, and skiing. She's better at some of these sports than others, but for Corrine, it's all about being with like-minded people who don't mind having a little fun.

LETTER TO READERS

Dear Reader,

We are honored that you have chosen to experience *Light in the Darkness: Uncovering Grief and Trauma* with us. Our hope is that you are now exploring, asking the questions, and doing the work to heal from your trauma. No matter where you are on this healing path, the fact that you are here with us is timely and you can help us #liftthestigma regarding mental illness.

Our mission at the Conscious Content Collective® is to educate and spread awareness on issues that matter to humanity. Mental wellness has never been more critical. Our prayer for you is to recognize you are in the right place at the right time to do so. We are learning that all is in divine order and when you start looking for that in your own life, you will connect the dots to see how you got here in this moment.

Lastly, we want you to know how grateful we are to have shared this time with you as you read, evolved, grew and hopefully had your own a-ha moments as you read this book. The path of the human journey can be extraordinary, painful, and joyous. Our unique divine blueprint contains everything we need. We hope you found inspiration in The Wisdom Well and have implemented some new healing practices as a result.

For more information about the humanitarian films, podcasts, shows, and books that Conscious Content Collective® has to offer, go to https://consciouscontent.org and join our mailing list for updates.

We truly believe you are the light in the darkness. It's time to share that with others.

Kimberly Resch and Brian Ross

MORE FROM CONSCIOUS CONTENT

Conscious Humanity Inc. is a 501(c)(3) not for profit and was founded by Brian Ross and Kimberly Resch, award-winning documentarians having global impact with their own business and receiving global recognition for their integrity and authenticity in telling the stories of those who might not otherwise have a voice. Their purpose in creating Conscious Humanity is to reach under-served populations that, for socioeconomic reasons might never have awareness brought to their plights.

Conscious Humanity wants to tell their stories and help them reach those who can make a difference in their lives. Your support allows us to bring light to those who need it most. Donations allow the ongoing production of the stories begging to be told. Your donation helps to develop the assets for our educational film library. This library will be given free of charge to those who need to hear these messages that would not otherwise have access. Your monetary gift changes lives and gives hope to those who need it most.

To donate, visit http://chimedia.org/donate.html

Our films:

Light in the Darkness

Tethered

A Rescue Story

The Workplace Garden

EcoSPEARS

Cause and Effect

Rescue Animals in Criminal Justice

Police Mental Health

What's Happening In the Ocean?

First Responder PTSD Awareness

MIRACLE

Compassion Fatigue

Uncertain Times

What We Know, What We Don't

Our podcasts:

Road 2 Remarkable

Conscious Conversations

Did You Know?

Follow us on:

Twitter
https://twitter.com/CContentMedia

Facebook
https://www.facebook.com/consciouscontentllc

Instagram:
https://www.instagram.com/conscious_cc/

YouTube:
https://www.youtube.com/channel/
UCw3sCPrHePluNo_6qaOqHUA

LinkedIn:
https://www.linkedin.com/company/consciouscontentllc

Our Website:
https://consciouscontent.org/get-involved/

ADVANCE PRAISE

As someone who knows and loves many who are first responders or in the military, I have seen firsthand how many people experience the pain of trauma. Knowing that these experiences change the brain is huge, absolutely huge! Knowing that no one needs to stay in that place of deepest pain and that support and healing is possible is powerfully heart-filling and frankly, quite exciting. I strongly encourage you to read this book for yourself and read it for those you love. It may well change your life as you understand and embrace a new level of healing.

—Sandy Walden, Grief Coach, Author of *The Acorn Journal, Messages of Connection from The Other Side*

Firefighters, law enforcement officers, and members of the military are very adept at training for crisis situations and adapting to dynamic circumstances. Still, we struggle mightily coping with associated mental anguish. "Light in the Darkness" is a must read for those who protect us as it demonstrates a great life is possible beyond the grief.

—Jim Etzin, Emergency Medical Services Coordinator, Oakland County (Michigan) Tactical Training Consortium

I have always believed that good art does not come from a happy place, and it lets the onlooker take from it what their soul needs in that moment. This book is art in its most crucial, incontestable, and heart-achingly deliberate form. It helps you realize not

only what your trauma looks like, but how to hold it so that it does not hurt you. Trauma and all the emotions that live within it are part of the human condition, yet an unfamiliar reality to many. Thank you for bringing these tools and resources together with empathy and precision.

—Kathy Velasquez, People Leader, Empath, Learner, Writer

"Light in the Darkness" is a beautiful integration of information, personal stories, and resources! As I read each chapter, I wiped tears and found myself nodding in agreement. This book is a gift for so many who are hurting and navigating their personal healing journeys. Kimberly and Brian, thank you for allowing yourselves to be vulnerable and share such raw emotions with us. Blessings to you both as you continue to do such critical and important work!

—Lisa Kelly, Intuitive Life Coach

After reading "Light in the Darkness," I discovered how the perception of darkness can be a multitude of tragic episodes. I am more determined and motivated to help as many individuals see the Light. Personally, I will address my uncovered sufferings from my very own experiences due to childhood and adulthood family death. Your book captured me in ways of direct reflections and is so authentic and heartfelt, plus healing! Thanks for providing unity, inspiration and healing through this profound and powerful book. For certain a must read!

—Jarvis Johnson, Social Entrepreneur

Amazing! This book is a phenomenal guide through all the complex emotions of PTSD and the healing journey for all involved.

—Khristi Kennedy Otto, DC

"Light in the Darkness" hits home on so many levels for me and I'm sure for many others. I had chills and held back tears while reading through it. There are some raw and real worlds contained within. This book reminds us we are absolutely a light in the darkness and the giver of hope to ourselves and others. "Light in the Darkness" will save lives!

—Marie Green, Mother and Wife

As a fire trauma survivor, "Light in the Darkness" helped me to feel not quite so alone. Until you experience trauma yourself, most people seem to think you should just "get over" it with time. That, I have learned, is not true. Life is forever "before the fire" and "after the fire" for me. Seeing that I am not alone in this is of great comfort.

—Sasha Mauck, SJM Financials, Inc.

The research and personal dialogues about various forms of mental illness in "Light in the Darkness" help to destigmatize mental illness. Each chapter concludes with "The Wisdom Well" which is filled with resources that the reader can explore. Thank you, Kimberly and Brian, for the courage to share your very personal journey and especially sharing your grief at the loss of Taylor.

—Paul A. Linzmeyer, Community and Business

Activist

Life is complex, and it comes with its own set of challenges. At any given point in our lives, trauma shows up unwillingly. The fight to get through trauma should never be done alone. It takes an immense amount of effort and community resources to help guide us to better understand our lives. This book highlights the importance of sharing our stories and the impact it has on others seeking a higher vibration. I highly recommend reading "Light in the Darkness" and sharing the light with those who need it.

—Corey Torres, Wellness Consultant,
    CoachCorey365 LLC

"Light in the Darkness" provides hope for recovery for those who have lived through pain and trauma. In reality, when a crisis happens, it exposes who we are and what we believe. I recommend "Light in the Darkness" because of its practicality in developing a personal strategy when walking through a trauma trail. This is a much-needed light to the path.

—Dwight Bain, Nationally Certified Counselor and
    founder of The LifeWorks Group

"Light in the Darkness" is a compelling, eye-opening, raw, and authentic compilation of personal experiences of trauma and how those experiences have affected individuals, families, and generations. As an expert in family and business psychology, I see the way patterns are passed down through the generations. I recognize that each individual's experiences impact much more than the present day. I believe this book will shed light on the

stigma of the mental health issues that are rooted in trauma and the lasting effects these experiences can have. I have the utmost respect for each person who had the courage to share their story, and wish for healing and brighter days for all. I encourage anyone looking for strength and trying to find peace to read this book!

—Anjali Seefeldt, MA, CFBA, Strategic Solutions Consulting

Deep, raw, and essential. This perfectly balanced book comes from a place of true vulnerability and passion. You can truly feel that the authors genuinely care, not only for the subject matter, but for each and every reader individually. Highly recommended!

—Brett Hensley, Veteran, Success Coach, President of Campfire Real Estate Group

As someone who is an empath and very aware of my PTSD and is on my own journey of healing/learning coping mechanisms, I felt connected with so many of the brave people who shared their experiences. I also enjoyed the book's little treasure trail of inspirational quotes so much that I promised my friend who also suffers from PTSD that I would send her a copy of this book. So many people think that medication is the end all be all to mental health issues, and while that may help some, the resources in this book opened my eyes to a whole new enlightening world of holistic and spiritual healing that is not whacky but instead loving, centered and down to earth, and completely attainable.

—Amanda Rudd, Amanda Cupcake, Sugar Therapist

Wow. Just wow. For anyone who has dealt with anxiety, this book will help give you tools. As a survivor with PTSD, this is quite eye opening and enlightening. It's relatable and reassuring to realize we are all human and acknowledging our minds can be as fragile as our bodies was profound for me. It's encouraging that the experiences of others have been shared so openly confirming we aren't crazy for feeling how we do. This book brought me to a place of 'finally' feeling there is hope!

—Jennifer Duquette, Internal Account Specialist

As a journalist with PTSD, my experiences resonate with the testimonies found in this book. It is real and relatable. Like so many with PTSD, I have my own experiences with trauma. As a journalist, covering tragedy after tragedy in my profession has left its impact on my life. This book gives you tools to help yourself heal from your trauma. It's comforting to know I'm not alone."

—Marcella Raymond, Journalist

The experiences, research, and learnings in this book give deep insight and direction for the grieving souls that have painful memories and are challenged by PTSD and mental illness. There is hope.

—Judy Green, CEO Emeritus Shareholder / Director Premier Sotheby's International Realty

Kim, I'm so proud of you. This book is absolutely your legacy to the entire world. You have literally put your heart and soul into

this project. Reading the raw pain of grief that you have documented is gut-wrenching for me. It's a pain that I am helpless to "kiss and make it better" for you. As your mother, I can't protect you from this, and that breaks my heart. I know that in the messages I get from Taylor that he is at peace and is surrounding all of us with the light of his love. He is bursting with pride for you. I'm so very proud of you for digging deep into your inner strength and carrying this tremendous feat to fruition. I knew from the second you were born that you would become an exceptionally amazing human being. Congratulations on a job well done. I love you.

—Kimberly Resch's mom, Dawn Carlson

I am quite sure this book can give comfort to many people out there who lost a loved one and are not able to cope with grief. I can recommend this book because this topic hits us all sooner or later.

—Gabi Ruggieri, Pax Svc Sup American Naval Air Base Sigonella, Founder Ohana Dream

This deserves 10 out of 5 stars. This is a must-read from grade school teachers to law enforcement leaders and everyone in between. It sheds much-needed light onto a dark topic that is easily brushed to the side. This message needs to be shared more than ever. You can feel the author's passion and their love and dedication that was poured into this project.

—Jeff Veal, Host of Blast Talks Podcast: Putting Real Life Stories on Blast